'Time-Journeys' –
A Counter-image to
Anthroposophical Spiritual Research

'Time-Journeys' –
A Counter-image to
Anthroposophical Spiritual Research

*A Presentation for Members of
the Anthroposophical Society*

Sergei O. Prokofieff

**Wynstones
Press**

Published by
Wynstones Press
Stourbridge
England.

www.wynstonespress.com

First English edition 2013

Originally published in German under the title *'Zeitreisen'* –
ein Gegenbild anthroposophischer Geistesforschung by
Verlag am Goetheanum, Dornach, in 2013
(edited by Ute E. Fischer).

Translated from the German by Willoughby Ann Walshe.
Edited by Thomas O'Keefe.

© Verlag am Goetheanum.
This translation © Wynstones Press.

The moral right of the author has been asserted under
the Copyright, Design and Patents Act, 1988.

All rights reserved. No part of this publication may be
reproduced, stored in a retrieval system, or transmitted, in any form
or by any means, electronic, mechanical, photocopying or otherwise,
without the prior permission of the publishers.

Cover layout based on original design by
© Walter Schneider www.schneiderdesign.net

Printed by Cambrian Printers, Aberystwyth.

ISBN 9780 946206 74 2

*Rudolf Steiner's pastel sketch from 1915 for the central motif
of the painting in the small cupola of the first Goetheanum.*
© *Goetheanum Art Collection*

This sketch represents the relation between the crucified Jesus
and the Risen Christ in the Mystery of Golgotha.

This presentation is based on a report that I gave on
24 November 2010 in the Goetheanum regarding the same
theme, at the request and within the circle of the Collegium
[Leadership] of the School for Spiritual Science.

CONTENTS

Introduction: Clearing Some Misconceptions   9

I.   A Personal Testimony of J. v. Halle
and Its Influence on Her Supporters   13

II.   The Method of Anthroposophical Spiritual Research
and Its Counter-image in 'Time-Journeys' and
Body-bound Visions   25

III.   Contradictions to Rudolf Steiner   39

Appendices

1.   Comments Regarding the Book by P. Tradowsky   97

2.   An Incorrect Reference to Rudolf Steiner   115

3.   The Assessment of J. v. Halle by a Tombergian   123

Notes   127

Bibliography   153

Introduction
Clearing Some Misconceptions

The information and rumours regarding my standpoint towards Judith von Halle, which have been launched in wide circles of the Anthroposophical Society and beyond in recent years, prompt me to correct some of that here.

As a member of the Vorstand of the General Anthroposophical Society, I want to state clearly from the start that I fully respect all of J. v. Halle's rights as a member of the Anthroposophical Society and of the School for Spiritual Science, including her right to act as a speaker in branches of the Anthroposophical Society and as an author.

I would also like to emphasize that I have never sought contact with J. v. Halle, because for me there is no need to meet her in person or to get to know her better. What I am solely interested in is the content that she has been presenting for many years in the form of lectures and books for the anthroposophical public.

Every public presentation creates a public effect. This makes possible that the listeners and readers can bring forward objective criticism of the contents presented, in the sense that they can test whether the respective statements are sufficiently justified or should be refuted.

This is absolutely correct, and is a fundamental practice in the scientific-academic world. For one publishes books so that they will be read, and the reader is free to accept or reject their content; or, in the event that errors are discovered, to correct them, and indeed to do so in full public view. To do just that is one of the purposes of this publication, and the same applies to several other critical reviews that have meanwhile appeared[1] concerning texts by J. v. Halle.

J. v. Halle's private life is her personal matter and does not interest me. In my view this includes all physical markings that can appear on a person, as well as a person's relation to taking in nourishment. Most assuredly, in the Catholic Church there have been and still are many people who bear various markings on their body and are able to have visions or something similar pertaining to the life of Jesus. But I must confess that I am not interested in such phenomena at all, because out of anthroposophy and out of my own inner experience, I know that Christ must be sought and found today solely in spirit. For it is precisely this relation that constitutes the primary signature of our time – a time in which Christ acts among humanity in etheric form. All physical manifestations, of any kind whatsoever, do not pertain to this.

In this respect one can share the opinion of Richard Pollak – an anthroposophist and esoteric pupil of Rudolf Steiner – who regarded his physical markings (stigmata) as belonging to the past and not to the anthroposophical path of schooling, and was fully supported in this judgment by Rudolf Steiner, with whom he had spoken about this.[2]

Additionally, it does not concern me whether J. v. Halle takes in nourishment or does not require it. I am aware that the phenomenon of living without nourishment exists in the world and assumes various different forms (but in all cases without guaranty). For example, there are people in the Anthroposophical Society who, in their own way, really or allegedly practice living without taking in nourishment. One of these has even written a book about this.[3] Otherwise, one meets this phenomenon particularly with some fakirs and yogis in the East, and less often in some Christian saints. But I must confess that this also is not of interest to me.

Naturally, there are yet further so-called wonder-phenomena in the world and among people that cannot be explained by present-day science. I can well imagine that curious and sensationally inclined people are greatly interested in these things. But even then I do not share this interest. Why not? It is because in this life I have committed myself only to Rudolf Steiner's spiritual science. This has nothing to do with wonder-phenomena or any kind of magical manipulations, but solely and strictly with scientifically founded knowledge of the spiritual world, which is rooted in the development of sense-free thinking. To guard, to teach, and if possible to further advance this spiritual-scientific knowledge is the central task of the members of the Anthroposophical Society founded by Rudolf Steiner in 1923.

When I recognized the central importance of Rudolf Steiner's spiritual science for our time, I became a member (1977) of the community of people who are united in their commitment to cultivating this spiritual science. According to my abilities, I strive to promote precisely this activity within the Anthroposophical Society. Briefly stated, in the Anthroposophical Society I seek only Rudolf Steiner's anthroposophy and those people who also feel committed to it in this way.

Therefore it is a mystery to me why, ever and again, the demand is made that within the Anthroposophical Society one must occupy oneself with various 'wonder-phenomena' (such as physical markings or living without nourishment). I find this unwarranted and must, for the above-mentioned reasons, reject this demand – for it in no way pertains to the tasks of this Society.

Therefore, I would like to take this opportunity clearly to dismiss all allegations that I have a personal antipathy towards J. v. Halle or that there could exist a bad karma between us. For me, especially the latter idea belongs to the completely unfounded fantasies of people of a not entirely healthy state of soul. With such suggestions, what should be an objective discussion of the contents of J. v. Halle's books (as is striven for in what follows) is dragged down to a personal level – where it, however, in no way belongs, and through which the atmosphere within the Anthroposophical Society as a cognitive community is unnecessarily poisoned.

I would also like to emphasize that I have composed the following observations not without a heavy heart. However, I recognize it as my responsibility towards anthroposophy, and also towards Rudolf Steiner, to take this step. Thus, the following presentations have not arisen from short-term considerations, but from my forty-four years of intensive and meditative involvement with anthroposophy and especially anthroposophical Christology, to which my hundreds of lectures and dozens of books testify.

At the end of this introduction, it should be mentioned that I made the decision to print this publication after the appearance of P. Tradowsky's book *Stigmatisation. Ein Schicksal als Erkenntnisfrage* [In English: *The Stigmata. Destiny as a Question of Knowledge*[4]], which was directed against me. The present book can therefore be considered as an answer to it.

So that my refutation of P. Tradowsky's statements is more comprehensible for the reader, it will be preceded by a general presentation of my position with respect to J. v. Halle's 'time-journeys' and the contents portrayed therein.

I.

A Personal Testimony of J. v. Halle and Its Influence on Her Supporters

In my view, one cannot truly understand the phenomenon of J. v. Halle and its influence on her supporters unless one takes note of a particular testimony written by her. For her whole soul-configuration is revealed with stunning clarity in a personal testimony from 2004 (at which time, as she reports, her physical markings appeared).

First, a brief summary of the history of this personal testimony. To begin with, in 2004, it was sent internally as part of a letter from J. v. Halle to the Vorstand in Dornach as well as to the Leading Council of the German national Society; therefore, it initially remained a statement to be respected as private, which as a member of the Vorstand one could only take note of with a certain uneasiness. Later, this personal testimony was also made public in the course of the Berlin conflict (in all likelihood with J. v. Halle's full consent). In 2007, in order to appease the conflict that had arisen in Berlin, the Anthroposophical Society in Germany called to life a so-called Mediation Commission, which was to conclude its work with an official report about the Berlin problem.

In the commission's official report, statements were made by all parties involved in the conflict; among these was, of course, also J. v. Halle. This commission report would then later be sent to all members of the Anthroposophical Society in

Germany as a basis for forming a judgment for the upcoming annual meeting. However, before the text of the commission report was finally made public, it was sent to all authors involved so that they could have the possibility to read their contributions once more, and if necessary to correct facts, omit parts, or formulate changes. Naturally, this applied also to J. v. Halle. Therefore, she had the chance in the last minute to remove or at least modify the personal testimony that she had contributed as her part of the report. She did not do this, and consequently her personal testimony was made public.

Accordingly, it appeared in the document 'Zusammenfassung des Abschlussberichts der Urteils-Findungs-Kommission über den Verlauf der Berliner Krise 2003 bis 2006' [Summary of the Final Report of the Judgment-Finding Commission regarding the Course of the Berlin Crisis from 2003 to 2006] in 'Materialien zur Mitgliederversammlung 2007' [Materials for the General Meeting of 2007] within the 'Mitteilungen aus der anthroposophischen Arbeit in Deutschland' [Newsletter of the Anthroposophical Work in Germany] No. 4/2007, which, as mentioned above, was sent to all members of the Anthroposophical Society in Germany.

Inasmuch as J. v. Halle's self-testimony was published in unchanged form, I allowed myself to have it reprinted in the weekly magazine *Das Goetheanum* in an open letter to Dietrich Rapp, as my response to the criticism that he had previously published there regarding the Appendix 'The Forces of the Phantom and Stigmatization' in my book *The Mystery of the Resurrection in the Light of Anthroposophy*.[5] Because most readers probably do not know the content of my open letter to Dietrich Rapp or no longer have it in mind, I would like once more to bring it to awareness here. For the reader will find in it not only the self-testimony of J. v. Halle in question (printed in italics in the letter), but also some of my thoughts concerning it, which are just as valid today as when they first appeared.

*

An Open Letter to Dietrich Rapp

Dear Dietrich Rapp,

    With these lines I would like to reply to some statements in your review.*

---

* As an explanation for English readers, the following should be mentioned at this point: In 2008, my book *Das Mysterium der Auferstehung im Lichte der Anthroposophie* appeared in the Stuttgart publishing house Verlag Freies Geistesleben. (This book is available in English translation as *The Mystery of the Resurrection in the Light of Anthroposophy*, Temple Lodge 2010, and will also appear in Dutch translation at the end of 2013.) Two reviews of it were later published in the weekly newsletter *Das Goetheanum*, No. 6/2009: a positive one by Heinz Zimmermann, who was at that time a member of the Vorstand; and a critical one by the former editor of the newsletter, Dietrich Rapp.

    The latter review was concerned less with the contents of the book itself than its Appendix: 'The Forces of the Phantom and Stigmatization'. In this Appendix, I attempted to clarify the phenomenon of physical blood-markings from a spiritual-scientific point of view. For this, I took as an example the German stigmatic and visionary Anna Katharina Emmerich, who lived at the beginning of the nineteenth century. Dietrich Rapp's criticism was directed primarily against the contents of this Appendix. This is because he thought that by characterizing Anna Katharina Emmerich's visions I really meant not her, but Judith von Halle. (See my remarks later on in this chapter.)

    Additionally, a particular resentment was brought against me because I had also presented Rudolf Steiner's statements with

15

In the criticism that you express here – namely that in my 'Appendix' I did not mention the name Judith von Halle – there is in my view a misunderstanding of the objective that I connect with this Appendix. In it I have referred to the phenomenon of stigmatization and the related 'time-journeys' in-and-of themselves, and characterized these as objectively as possible. In this connection, and in order to avoid unnecessary emotionalism, I have cited examples of reports about time-journeys from stigmatized people who are not our contemporaries (for Judith von Halle is certainly not the only stigmatized person at present). On this basis, I wanted to refrain from involving Judith von Halle directly, and thereby to raise the entire matter to a higher, suprapersonal level. I myself would not have anything against my books being treated objectively in this way – without direct reference to them and without mentioning my name, and if necessary also critically. I consider such an approach entirely fair.

However, the fact that many readers bring my presentations into connection with Judith von Halle's person is provided

---

regard to Anna Katharina Emmerich in my Appendix. Rudolf Steiner says in these statements, among other things, that Emmerich was 'an exceptionally good somnambulist'. (This statement can be found in the 'Answers to Questions' about the lecture cycle *Ägyptische Mythen und Mysterien* [*Egyptian Myths and Mysteries*] (GA 106), which are not yet published in the complete edition of Rudolf Steiner's work.) In order to respond to Dietrich Rapp's critical remarks, I answered them with an open letter in the next issue of *Das Goetheanum*.

In this context it was especially important to me to place Judith von Halle's self-testimony, which in the meantime had become publicly known, once again in the centre of the discussion of her person and work. *For unless one becomes aware of this self-testimony, it is impossible to form an objective judgment about her activity and the effect she has on her supporters.*

for, among others, by Wolfgang Garvelmann's book *Sie sehen Christus. Anna Katharina Emmerick, Therese Neumann, Judith von Halle ... Eine Konkordanz* [They See Christ. ... A Concordance], which was published by the Verlag am Goetheanum along with all of Judith von Halle's books – as well as the Afterword that she composed for her book *Das Abendmahl* [The Last Supper]. In this Afterword, Judith von Halle likewise attempts, by means of a concrete example, to emphasize the similarity between her visions and those of Katharina Emmerich.

In the Appendix of my book, I have undertaken a spiritual-scientific presentation of the phenomenon described above, which has accompanied the history of a part of Christian humanity throughout centuries. With the comparison of two contemporaries – Novalis, as a true Christian initiate and direct forerunner of anthroposophy,[6] and Katharina Emmerich, a visionary inclined to somnambulism – it should become evident where the boundaries lie, in the past as well as today, between Rudolf Steiner's spiritual science and the various forms of spiritual experiences and visions that are foreign to it. For in this case, Rudolf Steiner's silence about Katharina Emmerich is just as telling as his many lectures about Novalis. This silence clearly indicates what occult stream Rudolf Steiner did not want to have his anthroposophy mixed with. These examples from the nineteenth century should show what spiritual paths lead to anthroposophy and which do not. Furthermore, I cannot comprehend why one of Rudolf Steiner's statements about Katharina Emmerich, and my attempt to understand this from a spiritual-scientific perspective, should not be discussed in an anthroposophical context!

With my book, I did not intend to write a polemical work directed against someone personally. Therefore, I felt there was no reason for me to mention Judith von Halle's name in the Appendix. However, because I am compelled to do so by your review, I will do this in the form of an 'open letter' and present in the following what I currently see as the main problem regarding Judith von Halle. However, for the reasons presented here, I must decidedly reject your accusation that I have written 'a dishonest book'.

In my Appendix, I have expressed my own conviction and made an attempt to demonstrate its validity from a spiritual-scientific point of view. I do not compel anyone to share this judgment. Everyone is free to follow my exposition – or not. And of course, I fully and completely respect that there are people who have a different opinion about this issue. Certainly every person should gain his own impression; but at the same time, one must accept that there can be different judgments about the same phenomenon, whereby everyone is free to find one or the other viewpoint more convincing. In no way can one, in your words, speak here of 'anathematization'. Rather, as with any debate about questions of a spiritual nature, so in this case should mutual respect for freedom of opinion be the rule.

What in my view leads to a real problem is that on the basis of her stigmatization and visions, Ms. von Halle lays claim to an enormous spiritual authority. In this connection, shortly after her stigmatization occurred and her 'time-journeys' began, she communicated the following in a circular letter, dated September 2004, to representatives of regional centres of the Anthroposophical Society in Germany as well as to the Vorstand and the Collegium of the School for Spiritual Science at the Goetheanum:

'Please look upon me not as a person to whom a seemingly inexplicable miracle has occurred. Please consider the spiritual facts

that underlie this phenomenon. Any presentation of these events should not place my person in the foreground. Because these events happen to me, they are linked with my being. But it is always Christ Himself Who speaks to you personally – lovingly – when you concern yourself with this stigmatization-event that has occurred within the Anthroposophical Society – in that He, through His grace, through the guidance and support of your karma, allows you yourself to become witness to His passage through the earthly world, to His authenticity, to His omnipresence.'

The final sentence of this personal testimony speaks for itself. For me, such a claim is the end of anthroposophy. Never in all of spiritual history have any saints, stigmatized persons, or popes put forward such a claim.

The words cited above were reinforced in a second circular letter, undersigned by Judith von Halle among others, containing the further claim: Judith von Halle bears the Phantom of the Risen Christ.[7] This presumption also appears to me to make nearly impossible any free and independent discussion about the contents of her later writings and lectures.

Herein lies the answer to your other criticisms. It is self-evident that our Anthroposophical Society is open for all existing streams that are connected with Michael and his supersensible School – not, however, for claims of this nature. For through such claims an element is brought into anthroposophy that exerts a strongly suggestive effect – that restricts individual freedom, and that is therefore alien to the very essence of anthroposophy.

Thus, it seems to me that your comparison with Theodora from Rudolf Steiner's *Mystery Dramas* is unfounded. She is neither stigmatized nor does she report about 'time-journeys'. She also has no intention of broadcasting herself or seeking recognition in the way shown above. She simply relates how the

Christ can be experienced in the present age, as well as how – in accord with what Rudolf Steiner described – from our time on, this experience will become increasingly prevalent for the whole of humanity, a development for which anthroposophy will provide a necessary foundation. In the *Mystery Dramas*, Theodora is an example of modesty and discretion.

I also cannot follow your comment about the 'Gnostic Platonizing tendency' which you believe to have found in my book. For Rudolf Steiner emphasized very particularly that the Resurrection body could not be seen with physical eyes (otherwise Mary Magdalene would have recognized the Risen One immediately). Nowhere in Rudolf Steiner's work have I read that one can see something in the spiritual world with physical eyes. So I hope that readers of my book will recognize for themselves from out of its contents the decisive importance of the physical body. For I wrote this book in order to make the Resurrection of the body, based on Rudolf Steiner's spiritual research, more comprehensible for people of today.

I would be willing to respond to your further accusations, but that would go beyond the editorial boundaries for this letter. For readers truly interested in this subject, I would recommend they read the passages cited from my book in their full context.

With kind regards,
Sergei Prokofieff

P.S. Thank you for drawing attention to the printing mistake on page 181 in my book.

*

In the next issue of *Das Goetheanum*, J. v. Halle answered my open letter quite sharply. It was for me particularly significant that in response, she did not bring into question or change a single word of her self-testimony. With this, she has once more publicly confirmed that she remains fully connected with it.

This being clearly the case, I would here like to express openly that I regard this statement of J. v. Halle as a blasphemous pretension. For the path to Christ today forms itself – and the whole of anthroposophy speaks for this – in a fully individual way, as a pure meeting of the human 'I' with the World-'I' of Christ, without any mediation through another person. To presume on any ground whatsoever that due to physical markings one is oneself such a mediator, and this on the deepest karmic level, is an entirely unjustifiable claim.[8] Even when the Catholic Church insists on assuming such a mediating role between Christ and humanity, it does so not through an individual personality, but rather solely through the Church in its entirety.

Especially in our time, such forms of mediation (through a single person or an earthly institution) are completely inappropriate; for in the era of the etheric reappearance, Christ will increasingly reveal Himself to human beings in His eternal presence – however only in an entirely personal way and without any outer mediation.

There is yet another reason why I must attach such weight to J. v. Halle's statement cited above. For let us imagine that someone would completely accept her self-testimony and take it for an unconditional truth; that is what many of her supporters do – from their ranks a critical remark has never been voiced in this regard. Then the person who believes this statement – for here it is indeed no longer a question of knowledge, but rather of belief – could only 'throw himself at the feet' of J. v. Halle in the naïve belief of having found in her the proposed mediator to Christ. When such a thing happens, then we are dealing with a stream of pure belief within the Anthroposophical Society, through which questions of knowledge give way to the content of belief.

I have come to learn that there actually are such supporters of J. v. Halle, on the basis of various letters filled with great fanaticism and genuine hatred towards me. For in the eyes of her faithful supporters I am, due to my critical remarks, not merely an opponent of J. v. Halle; rather they also see in me – so I have to feel it – an opponent of Christ Himself. Otherwise hateful letters of this nature would not be written to me, which presumably have their source in a feeling of needing to come to the defence of Christ.

In this way, belief in the content of the personal testimony cited above gives rise to a division in our Society with purely religious roots. This is why an objective discussion of J. v. Halle's statements and writings, which within the Anthroposophical Society should take place solely on the level of knowledge, has been impossible from the outset. In reality we stand today in the midst of a war of belief, through which people are divided into those who believe in J. v. Halle's self-testimony and those who must reject it for the reasons mentioned.

It is therefore not surprising that much talk of a division within the Anthroposophical Society comes precisely from the circles around J. v. Halle. For instance, P. Tradowsky writes in his book *Und das Licht schien in die Finsternis...* [And the Light Shines in the Darkness...]: 'Within anthroposophical circles there is shown, on one hand, a profound receptivity to authentic presentations; and on the other hand, a lack of understanding, rejection, criticism, and even hostility. It has come to a more or less hidden polarization, to separations with the tendency towards division' (p. 106).[9]

The extent to which J. v. Halle is deified within her circles becomes apparent by the fact that in the same book, P. Tradowsky brings Rudolf Steiner's predicted culmination of anthroposophy around the turn of the century – from the twentieth to the twenty-first century – directly into connection with J. v. Halle's emergence: 'The spirit-light of the culmination of anthroposophy has been covered over by the darkness of the twentieth century; whether the culmination will make its appearance later and in another form is to be hoped for, and remains to be seen. The extraordinary spirit-light that appears in the individuality and destiny of J. v. Halle encounters the darkness of the decadence of the present time, but also that of incomprehension and rejection' (ibid., pp. 106-107).

II.
The Method of
Anthroposophical Spiritual Research
and Its Counter-image in
'Time-Journeys' and Body-bound Visions

In her first book, '*Und wäre Er nicht auferstanden...*' *Die Christus-Stationen auf dem Weg zum geistigen Menschen* [In English: *And If He Had Not Been Raised... The Stations of Christ's Path to Spirit Man*], published by J. v. Halle together with P. Tradowsky, the author describes rather precisely how she has come to the content of her body-bound visions. She presents their emergence and distinct physical-sensory character as follows: 'As you know, there is no historical proof for the life, ministry, death and Resurrection of Christ. It seems to be the case, however, that ever and again throughout the development of world history it is provided that there are individuals who, through a *sensory witnessing* of these events, are themselves able to be a living testimony for the fact of the Son of God' (pp. 31-32 G [p. 21 E], italics added).*

The amazing thing about this statement is that J. v. Halle does not describe herself as someone who provides a testimony about something, but she characterizes herself as a 'living testimony to the fact of the Son of God'. And further, 'Their

---

* Quotations are newly translated from the German edition. 'G' indicates original German edition; 'E' indicates the corresponding page in the English edition, when available. Ed.

perceptions [those people who attain to a sensory witnessing of the events at the time of Christ] are more comprehensive than any traditional document could ever be, and even more detailed than the Gospels, because this concerns, as I said, *actual sensory perceptions*. Reports are known about this from other stigmatics. *... When I therefore speak of sensual perceptions, that is exactly what is meant.* I can speak to you now from my own experience: Imagine that you undertake a time-journey, with the result that with your daily waking consciousness and all of the perceptive capabilities you possess while you sit here in the auditorium and hear my voice, see the curtain behind me, maybe smell the cleaning detergent of the floor, feel the arm of your neighbour – that with all of these faculties of perception, you are transferred to another time' (ibid., p. 32 G [pp. 21-22 E], italics added).

This self-testimony, as well as other descriptions in the book, indicates that we are here concerned with physically-bound sensory perceptions, which due to a 'time-journey' are set back about 2,000 years. This would be as if one were able to look through a keyhole into the room of the Last Supper, listening to the people there speak to each other in Aramaic, smelling the food and spices that they eat, and seeing with one's own physical eyes certain details in the environment and furnishings of the room. From this it is clear that we are speaking about perceptions that are only mediated through the physical senses, be they from the present or the distant past. In another book, she describes it thus: 'It may be imagined as a type of "time-journey", in which we are present with all sensory impressions that we can have through our present-day waking consciousness – only transferred to a particular time and place' (*Das Mysterium des Lazarus...*, p. 10).[10]

It is precisely the body-bound character of such sensory perceptions that stands in stark contrast to what Rudolf Steiner

26

gave as the modern path of anthroposophical schooling. For on this path, sensory cognition, which is given to all people, forms only the preliminary stage to actual spiritual cognition. In his book *The Stages of Higher Knowledge*, Rudolf Steiner designates it as the 'material mode of cognition'.[11] This has nothing to do with spiritual cognition in the anthroposophical sense, which comprises the stages of Imagination, Inspiration and Intuition.

This very first material stage of cognition, which Rudolf Steiner describes at the same time as 'ordinary and sensory-scientific' (ibid.) consists of 'four elements'. He characterizes them as follows: '... 1. *the object*, which makes an impression upon the senses; 2. *the image*, which the human being forms of this object; 3. *the concept*, through which the human being arrives at a spiritual comprehension of an object or an event; 4. *the "I"*, which forms for itself the image and concept based on the impression of the object' (ibid., italics Rudolf Steiner). And regarding the last element, he says further: 'The fourth element that comes under consideration in material cognition is the "I". In it, the union of images and concepts is produced. The "I" preserves the images in its memory' (ibid.).

All four elements share a common ground in their connection to the first element. In his further presentation, Rudolf Steiner also calls it 'sensation'. Everything that the human being perceives through his senses, he carries within himself as memory-images. With these he connects his thoughts, which themselves correspond to these images; that is, a person's thoughts are directed to sensory impressions and brought into connection with them. The necessary work for this is carried out by the 'I', which completely opens itself to the outer world and thereby becomes a part of it. In summary, one can say: First we are concerned with sensory perceptions, then with images that retain the sense-impressions, and finally with the sense-bound thinking and the 'I', which through this process of 'material cognition' is completely oriented to the sense-world, and thereby remains bound to the body.

Next Rudolf Steiner describes the transition from this beginning stage, where a person is still caught up in sense-impressions, to the first stage of supersensible cognition, the stage of Imagination. To achieve this, one must first and foremost suppress any connection to the sense organs and their activity. 'Meditation, concentration and other exercises bring it about that the soul withdraws for a time from its union with the sense organs.' For 'instead of "sensation", something else must appear in its place. This something is Imagination … *Here the senses remain entirely inactive*' (ibid., italics added). It is for this reason that a person already at the stage of Imagination must voluntarily renounce all sense-impressions and, through his exercises, extinguish them completely. For only by fulfilling this main precondition can he enter the Imaginative world consciously.[12]

However, in order truly to be able to live in this world, not only is the absolute renunciation of the activity of the physical senses required, but also the complete transformation of all other elements of 'material cognition'. All memory-images that still adhere to the senses must be removed from the soul during the meditative exercise. Likewise, thoughts associated with sense-impressions must be transformed so that they become sense-free and thus free of the body.[13]

Finally, the 'I' itself must experience a complete inner reorientation. During the time of meditation, it must strip away everything that somehow connects it with the physical-sensory world and its sense-impressions. Through the corresponding exercises, the 'I' reaches a state in which it can remain fully conscious without the consciousness being supported by sense-impressions, memory-images or body-bound thoughts.

Only when this state has been reached can a person on the modern path of schooling cross the threshold to the spiritual world *consciously* and meet the Guardian, in order thereby to gain admission from him into the objective spiritual world. Here, however, the person of today faces the real danger of losing himself at this threshold. For when he consciously leaves behind everything that lives in him as sense-impressions, memory-images, and body-bound thoughts and concepts, which comprise a substantial part of the content of his earthly 'I', what then remains left of this 'I'? Will it be capable of maintaining body-free consciousness in the midst of this pure emptiness?

Only when this is the case has the soul sufficiently prepared itself to cross the threshold to the spiritual world and to meet the strict requirements of the Guardian. These consist in the condition that within the human soul nothing, but absolutely nothing that in some way remains attached to the bodily senses and their impressions may be admitted by the Guardian into the spiritual world. And because a person's ordinary 'I' draws its content primarily from sense-impressions, it faces at the threshold the risk of losing everything, indeed, even itself.

Rudolf Steiner describes this situation as follows: 'When one reaches the Guardian of the Threshold, one must actually lay aside all that one knows of oneself. One must, however, still have something to carry oneself through it [pure, body-free 'I'-consciousness]. That is what matters! The fact that at this boundary one must leave everything behind, gives rise to an inner experience that one must be strong enough to face. And the preparation for this stage of clairvoyance must consist in – and does consist, in a correct inner schooling (with correct schooling one may not speak of dangers, because it is precisely a correct schooling that drives away the dangers) – learning to endure what would otherwise be dreadful and terrifying. Through this preparation one must come to be able to endure, for this endurance provides the fundamental power for all further experiencing' (GA 138, 27 August 1912).

And this means here that already in rising to the stage of Imaginative cognition, the spiritual pupil encounters the requirement of renouncing all sense-impressions as a basic condition. (To a still far greater extent, this is also the case for the further stages of Inspiration and Intuition.[14]) This renunciation, above all, is the precondition for encountering the Guardian and crossing the threshold consciously. Here one must not only remove from the soul, all the way into the soul's deepest individual fibres, the sense-impressions as such (this would have had to have happened previously); but additionally, all memories, thoughts and inclinations of the 'I' that still remain in some way attached to the physical-sensory world, or show even the slightest inclination to it, must disappear.

In what has here been said are truly to be found the most basic elements of the modern path of spiritual schooling – everything that each person must know who is somehow preparing to enter upon this path. For herein lies the very first stage, which builds the foundation for all that follow. Especially in the Class Lessons, Rudolf Steiner describes in detail and repeatedly the process of the human soul stepping outside of the body, which it must accomplish without being able to support itself by any sense-impressions, and yet while maintaining full 'I'-consciousness also outside the body. For that is the essence of this path.

Even from this brief overview, the reader can comprehend that the path of spiritual cognition communicated by

Rudolf Steiner to people of today runs in a diametrically-opposed direction to the sense- and body-bound 'time-journeys' that J. v. Halle presents as the basis for her spiritual experiences.

The tragedy in this is that at the outset, the co-author of her first book – and then she herself – brings her body-bound visions into connection with the activity of the Phantom of the Resurrected Christ, and thereby transfers her quite personal experiences to the Phantom. She writes: 'What is therefore the special feature of the Phantom in relation to the senses? One learns more about this phenomenon when one concentrates on the above-mentioned "expansion" of the senses. With the sense of smell there comes about a refinement, an expansion to such an extent that it is possible, for example, to identify the ingredients of creams, as well as food which someone else ate the previous day – or an increased iron level in the blood of another person, as the altered smell of his blood is perspired through the skin. The transformation of the sense of hearing is expressed not only in the supersensible perception of inspirational "tones" and soul-spiritual "sounds", but also, once again, in its extreme state of expansion. Thus, it can happen that one overhears conversations through doors, walls, and even in other houses' (*Und wäre Er nicht auferstanden...*, p. 50 G [p. 38 E]).

And then she speaks directly about her visual perceptions during 'time-journeys': 'The sensory-visual impression arises only through the physical-formative forces of the Phantom body. Therefore, any sense perception can take place over a distance of thousands of miles or even in another time' (ibid., p. 51 G [p. 38 E]).

Rudolf Steiner describes the Phantom as something completely different. It is that which actually exists in the world as the primal idea of the physical body: '... so likewise for the

31

human body is the primal idea at hand', which subsists 'as a real thought in the external world: as Phantom' (GA 131, 10 October 1911). In addition, he also calls the Phantom the 'spirit-body' (GA 131, 12 October 1911). From this it is clear that the Phantom of the Risen One has nothing to do with the sense organs and bodily perceptions 'expanding' their activities, but rather calls forth in the human being completely different and highly spiritual processes.

Even if J. v. Halle actually experiences the expansion of sense-impressions that she describes, there is in my view no reason to bring this into connection in any way with the Phantom of the Risen One.[15] If this association is made nevertheless, without any spiritual-scientific justification, then it leads in the same direction as J. v. Halle's self-testimony quoted in the previous chapter, namely to that of quite specially emphasizing the significance of her person and her body-bound visions, and to legitimizing them through her alleged relation to the Phantom.

*

A further related problem should be briefly discussed here. In February 2007, J. v. Halle gave a lecture under the auspices of the Section for the Literary Arts and Humanities in the Great Hall of the Goetheanum about Rudolf Steiner's wooden sculpture [The Representative of Humanity], with the title: 'The Working of Living Spirit-Beings in the Christ Statue'. Due to a physical impairment, she could not hold the lecture freely – as planned – but instead could only read it aloud while seated. This was the only lecture by J. v. Halle that I have attended. Later, the text of the lecture was published in the book 'Das Christliche aus dem Holze herausschlagen ...' Rudolf Steiner, Edith Maryon und *die Christus-Plastik* ['Hewing What is Christ-like from out of Wood ...' Rudolf Steiner, Edith Maryon and the Christ Statue], Dornach 2007.

The whole event made a very strange impression on me, for the following reason: To begin with, the speaker read for a fairly long time her presentation about Rudolf Steiner's Sculptural Group, which was interesting and at times even quite thought-provoking. In any case, her remarks certainly belong more to what anthroposophists refer to as secondary literature, that is, literature based on the continuation of Rudolf Steiner's foundational ideas: publications which are by now available from various anthroposophical publishing houses worldwide in such number that it is scarcely possible to get an overview of them all. The most essential characteristic of truly high-quality examples of such secondary literature is the condition – which Rudolf Steiner strictly required and also himself exemplified – that they can be cognitively understood by a healthy human understanding. By and large, this is how J. v. Halle presented her remarks.

In the course of further reading, however, the speaker made a pause, and then resumed suddenly (in my perception) with a change in facial expression and also no longer with the same voice. It was as if a different person were now speaking. And then followed, to my complete surprise, a gruesome story that had nothing to do with all the previous considerations, and which was also presented in such a way that there was no further possibility of drawing nearer cognitively to what was said (which in anthroposophical presentations should be the highest requirement).

She related that in a miraculous way, which must however remain mysterious, a few weeks before the Baptism of

Jesus in the Jordan River, three initiates of the black Mysteries had travelled to Palestine: one from India, another from Africa and a third from Central America. 'Each of them brought two things with him to Palestine: a piece of ore out of the region from which he came, and the quintessence of all black magic rituals from his region' (*Das Christliche aus dem Holze herausschlagen*, p. 49).

From this ore they cast – there were yet 'three further people [from Palestine] present, who brought iron as a fundamental material' (ibid.) – in a black-magical manner, three nails for His Cross; and this still before Christ came to Earth. During this time the working of evil was so intense that according to J. v. Halle's perception, the following was possible: 'One could smell the evil' (ibid.). The whole matter had the goal that, when fastened with these black-magic nails to the Cross, Christ Jesus would no longer have been able to Resurrect, and would thereby 'lose His divinity' (ibid., p. 51).

This dark goal is described by J. v. Halle as follows: 'Through the black-magic ritual [carried out by these three black magicians] each nail was imbued with a sorathic power which would ensure that the God Christ in the human body of Jesus would not come to death – that is, would not complete His earthly birth – and therefore could not have carried out the redemption of mankind; but instead would have had to remain imprisoned within the body of Jesus upon the wooden Cross. He should not achieve His divine mission of enlivening death, insofar as the nails would have firmly held the Divine Redeemer-Spirit within Jesus of Nazareth's flesh, so that He would have had to undergo death like all people in pre-Christian times, and thus fall prey to the influence of Ahriman. By this act, the God who came to make a sacrifice for humanity, which He Himself did not have need for, should lose His divinity and never be able to extend to His true glory and unlimited expanse. The Father was to have lost His Son, and with this, the whole human species' (ibid., pp. 50-51).

Here it seems that J. v. Halle has virtually no notion of the Phantom, which, in accordance with its restoration and liberation, could in no way be subject to the influence of any magical procedures with material objects (such as iron nails). For as 'spirit-body' (GA 131, 12 October 1911), the Phantom has in its archetypal origin and inner nature nothing to do with earthly materiality. Aside from this, it is a complete illusion to believe that simply through a few nails (even if they had been magically prepared) the Logos, Who is the Creator of the whole world, could 'lose His divinity'.

Then, according to J. v. Halle, there took place the very strangest thing: 'Three years later, precisely these nails were seized by the mercenary soldiers, by coincidence – they knew nothing of the peculiarity of these nails – in order to nail Christ to the Cross' (*Das Christliche aus...*, p. 50). And this occurred precisely so that the nail prepared by the Eastern magician was hammered into the left hand, the one by the Western magician into the right hand and the one by the Southern magician into the feet, for 'the Lord was to have been stretched in three directions over the Earth in the material sense, so that the Earth would become further materialized and not spiritualized' (ibid., p. 51). How one could think, on any grounds whatsoever, that with the Crucifixion of Christ Jesus a materialization of the Earth could have been accomplished, is beyond me. I think that a person who truly and thoroughly comprehends the whole cosmic-telluric dimension of the Mystery that took place on the Golgotha Hill, would never come to something like this.

When one hears or reads something like this, one is faced with a real problem. For given the complete absence of any verifiable knowledge, one can only *believe* this story – or not. This has nothing to do with the cognitive process in the anthroposophical sense; rather it brings us nearer the magical worlds of *The Lord of the Rings* or *Harry Potter*.

To this may be added the difficulty that in a brief introduction to this fairytale-like story, J. v. Halle mentions how she came to it. She says in this regard: '... and it is certainly helpful when one may have an impression of the sensible-supersensible conditions at the Turning Point of Time also through being able to speak out of the *sensory witnessing* of the events of that time' (ibid., p. 48, italics added). Immediately after this sentence in the book there follows a colon, and the author proceeds to recount the whole fantasy-story about the 'three dark kings' (p. 49). This sentence clearly proves that the emergence of this story has nothing, absolutely nothing to do with the anthroposophical path of schooling, which leads through Imagination, Inspiration and Intuition directly into the spiritual world; but on the contrary, the story is the result of precisely a 'sensory witnessing', as the perceptions within it are body-bound.

What is especially problematic in this whole context is that in the aforementioned lecture, and also in its published version, something is brought into connection with the presentation about the Sculptural Group – the presentation itself having been conducted thoroughly in the spirit of anthroposophy – that is in fact entirely foreign to this spirit. Through this, a seed of destruction is almost imperceptibly placed into the anthroposophical research-method.

*

In summary, it must once more be said that perhaps the worst part about this impenetrable mixture of body-bound visions, anthroposophical terminology and the results of Rudolf Steiner's research is the fact that in virtually all of J. v. Halle's books, anthroposophy together with its terminology is put to use in order to make her own visions quasi-'anthroposophical' and hence, believable to anthroposophical readers. She also uses direct citations from Rudolf Steiner toward this end, in no small measure. This, however, does not alter the fact that the source of her visions has nothing to do with anthroposophy itself and its research methods, nor with the results of Rudolf Steiner's research.

To this belongs something else that is entirely funda-mental: Because Anthroposophy is a being of the spiritual world,[16] she warrants selfless service, not an attempt to use her as a means to an end.

III.
Contradictions to Rudolf Steiner

As it is repeatedly heard from the circles of J. v. Halle's supporters that nowhere in the contents of her 'time-journeys' are the results of Rudolf Steiner's spiritual-scientific research contradicted, so this issue should also be dealt with here. Such a claim sounds even stranger after several such contradictions have been revealed in the book by Mieke Mosmuller, *Stigmata und Geist-Erkenntnis. Judith von Halle versus Rudolf Steiner* [Stigmata and Spirit-Cognition. Judith von Halle versus Rudolf Steiner].[17] The stir this book caused amidst J. v. Halle's supporters is quite understandable. In her extensive and thorough analysis (the book has 259 pages), M. Mosmuller compares a number of J. v. Halle's claims about the events surrounding the Mystery of Golgotha, which she says she saw with her own eyes during her 'time-journeys', with the corresponding results of Rudolf Steiner's research. Through this, a clear picture is given of the extent to which J. v. Halle's visions contradict the results of Rudolf Steiner's spiritual-scientific research.

Below I would like to present some additional instances where J. v. Halle contradicts Rudolf Steiner's statements, as well as a few of her visions, which when observed with healthy human understanding and from the standpoint of anthroposophy, lead of themselves to absurdity.

Because the contents of M. Mosmuller's book are perhaps unknown to some readers, we will begin with an example that M. Mosmuller has already presented in her book.

While reading J. v. Halle's book *Das Abendmahl. Vom vorchristlichen Kultus zur Transsubstantiation* [The Last Supper. From Pre-Christian Cultus to Transubstantiation] (Dornach 2006), I encountered the impossibility of the following assertion and the error of her description was immediately clear to me (even before reading M. Mosmuller's book). Therefore, I would like to start with this example.

It concerns Christ allegedly slaughtering a lamb before the Last Supper on Maundy Thursday. Here J. v. Halle follows, consciously or unconsciously, the ideas of A. K. Emmerich, who claims the same thing. Thereby, both do not notice that according to the Gospel of John the Jewish Passover took place on Good Friday, and thus Moses' law could not have been fulfilled the day before this. Also, according to Moses, slaughtering lambs should occur only in the temple.

At the very least, at this point anyone familiar with Rudolf Steiner's Christology would say: The true *Sun*-God, Who according to the testimony of the Letters to the Hebrews oriented His whole activity on the Earth in terms of the priesthood of Melchizedek's Sun Mysteries (See *Hebrews*, Chapter 7) – this means not in the service of the national-god Jahve, but in the sense of the Most High God El-eljôn, Whom Christ in His 'farewell discourses' (John 14-17) characterizes as the Father – could never perform a lunar blood-sacrifice in any form whatsoever. During the Last Supper, a determining moment in His life, something of His Sun-essence itself was transferred with the transformed bread and wine to the disciples – whereas in the Transfiguration on Mount Tabor Christ's higher Sun-nature became manifest only in the higher worlds. In this situation of the Last Supper, the moment at which the new Sun-humanity emerged, a lunar blood-sacrifice is absolutely unthinkable.[18]

Thus it is almost tragic when lately, especially in anthroposophical circles, the attempt is made to bring the Last Supper, with its deep relation to the Being of the Sun, into such a one-sided, retrogressive-lunar direction as is done in J. v. Halle's book *Das Abendmahl* [The Last Supper]. Moreover, in this publication the bloody character of the sacrifice is so strongly emphasized and placed into the foreground, that it is even asserted that Christ Himself carried out this bloody deed.[19]

The author further alleges that Christ slaughtered not only one lamb for His disciples, but also a second for the group of women, and this with a knife-incision in the throat: 'Since the cut was set with tremendous speed directly on the carotid artery, the animal died instantly, or was unconscious, before it could come to a sensation of pain' (pp. 50-51). And in just this manner Christ Jesus is said to have personally performed this deed with His own hands: 'on that evening in His capacity as teacher and Master, the Christ Jesus carried out the slaughter-incision with His own hands' (p. 51).

Thus, according to J. v. Halle, He extended this bloody event with a second Moon-sacrifice: 'After the slaughtering of the lamb, which was to be divided among the Lord and His disciples, the Redeemer carried out a second slaughter-incision: He slaughtered a lamb for the table of women' (p. 56). When J. v. Halle attempts to justify these two killings – 'He Himself slaughtered the lamb, since He would give of Himself as sacrifice' (p. 52) – this argument can be opposed forcefully: For precisely because Christ was the Lamb of God (John 1:36), He simply could not kill an earthly lamb nor did He have the need to put one to death.

Therefore, one must conclude that also in this instance, the visions of A. K. Emmerich and J. v. Halle simply do not correspond with the facts. Above all, J. v. Halle's bloody descriptions contradict everything that a Christ-seeking person can discover with the help of anthroposophy regarding the lofty Sun-event of the Last Supper.

Hence, one can agree entirely with Mieke Mosmuller's following statement regarding the description mentioned: 'Christ, as he is portrayed slaughtering lambs, is literally *unimaginable*; therefore these descriptions are altogether false. Even if yet thousands of stigmatics were to experience the same depiction – then they would all have made the same error.'[20]

In connection with J. v. Halle's allegation that she saw this bloody scene of the lunar sacrifice with her own physical eyes in her 'time-journeys' to the Turning Point of Time, the shock and inner aversion called forth by this depiction (for in reading this passage, I had much the same feeling as M. Mosmuller) raise the serious question: How can such a false perception even arise in the spiritual world? In the Appendix of my earlier book *The Mystery of the Resurrection in the Light of Anthroposophy*, I pointed out that in the case of such body-bound visions, in which one believes to have seen something spiritual with physical eyes, manifold errors are possible.[21]

Briefly summarized, the reason is not only the fact that such a seer has not come to her inner experiences through a genuine process of spiritual schooling (which is why she cannot ever really control her visions herself), but above all in the fact that it is not the true pictures from the Akashic Record that appear to her, but their multiply-distorted reflections in the Moon sphere. They are additionally influenced by the particular character of the Moon-realm, the content of which often arises as physical-sensory perceptions. For that reason alone they can only distort the real spiritual quality of given events and pull this quality down into the physical-sensory realm, which one may clearly observe from many of J. v. Halle's descriptions.[22]

Despite this explanation, the real question regarding the images – arising from body-bound visions – of such a bloody animal sacrifice in the midst of the Sun-like atmosphere of the Last Supper, is not yet answered. Therefore, something further should be contributed to solving this riddle. As already mentioned, the images of the Last Supper and other events of the Mystery of Golgotha, which can only be found in their purity in the Akashic Record[23] at the boundary between lower and upper Devachan[24] (where Rudolf Steiner researched them), also appear in mirror-image and in a sensory manner in the Moon sphere. There they are, however, scarcely possible to differentiate from other kinds of pictures that have been imprinted upon this sphere – especially through certain cult-like rituals – directly from the Earth.

One need only imagine how, for many centuries, thousands of lambs were slaughtered every year in the span of a few hours by priests in the great temple in Jerusalem for Passover, and how the stream of sacrificed animal blood would ever and again transport the people present into a state of ecstasy. For therein lies the actual purpose of the original blood sacrifice: to bring about a connection with the spiritual world in an ecstatic way. If one considers this together with how the whole process had been immensely enhanced by the corresponding cultic activities, ritualistic words and gestures that accompanied the slaughtering of animals – whereby the ecstatic feelings of the people present generated a tremendous soul-astral energy field – then one will understand that thereby this picture of the entirety of these events was imprinted with great intensity onto the Moon sphere. Therefore, this exceptionally strong picture of the blood sacrifice, ever and again nourished by astral forces, existed for centuries in the lunar region of the spiritual world adjacent to the Earth. From there it could penetrate the authentic images of the Last Supper stemming from above out of the Akashic Record, and thus produce an impenetrable mixture of accurate and false elements.

For the reasons mentioned there exists, especially for untrained seers who moreover cannot control their visions themselves, the real danger of confusing all manner of things with each other without having a clear notion of their completely different origin. That in regard to the Last Supper, J. v. Halle not only repeats A. K. Emmerich's mistakes, but enhances them still further and endows them with additional terrible details, is possibly due to the specific nature of her own visions.

Here is an example. At the end of her description of the Last Supper, J. v. Halle adds the following episode, which allegedly happened after the transformation of bread and wine into the body and blood of Christ and after the disciples' communion: 'From the chalice [of the Last Supper] containing what remained of the blood, He now poured this into the seventh cup,[25] into John's cup. Peter at His left gave a little wine, and John at His right gave a little water. *Therein the Redeemer washed His hands.* By washing His own hands, which were performing the ritual, in *His own body and blood,* He showed the disciples, without saying a word, that He voluntarily took upon Himself the sacrifice of His own being – that in a cosmic sense, He was not handed over by an arbitrary act of betrayal. *He then divided this blood among the six cups of the disciples, and they drank it*' (*Das Abendmahl,* pp. 99-100, italics added).

It took me some inner overcoming to quote this passage at all. I have done it, however, because the reader needs to know what grave matters are at issue here, and he should

44

also understand that the confrontation with the contents of J. v. Halle's 'time-journeys' reveals a very serious background. Therefore, I would suggest that the reader of the above description really once meditate these lines through with his healthy human feeling and understanding, in order to form his own judgment about this.

In reflecting on this, I have wondered how one would actually know of such rituals, in which hands are washed in the body and blood of a human being. Every learnèd person knows of such rituals from the black magic Mayan Mysteries, in which among other things the bodies of captured people were slashed open and the priests actually washed their hands in the blood-saturated entrails or other organs.

If one additionally considers that in points of crucial importance such as the Last Supper event, J. v. Halle ever and again incorporates incorrect images in her presentations – and the number of such instances could easily be increased from the content of her books[26] – then as a reader, one should take even more seriously Rudolf Steiner's urgent warning that an anthroposophist should be fundamentally 'suspicious' from the beginning of these and similar visions. His exact words were: 'Thus if a clairvoyant perception arises automatically, it is best not to say to oneself that one is a divinely gifted person to whom something has been given that one has not acquired [through a proper spiritual-scientific schooling]; for here it is best to be suspicious' (GA 161, 1 May 1915).

*

An evident contradiction, not only to Rudolf Steiner, but to the whole tradition of Christianity confirmed by him, comes to expression in J. v. Halle's claim that the Cross on Golgotha had a

Y-form instead of the world-renowned †-form. She reports as follows: 'The cross beams [of the Cross on the Golgotha Hill] were not quite horizontal to the trunk beam, but embedded into the prefabricated side holes of the main trunk like a Y' (*Und wäre Er nicht auferstanden...*, p. 78 G [p. 65 E]).[27]

The central idea of her statement as such is not new. As early as 200 years ago, another 'time-journeying' person, A. K. Emmerich, presented this theory – and she felt so strongly connected to it all throughout her life, that there was even erected on her grave in Dülmen, Germany, instead of a †-Cross, a Cross in the form of a Y, which presumably still stands there today. Both claim to have seen this Y-form on the Golgotha Hill with their own physical eyes. From this they draw the final authenticity of their visions, as well as their unshakeable conviction of the truth of what they have seen. For how should one doubt what one has indeed seen with one's own eyes? Both (actually there were three, for T. Neumann also saw this[28]) needed a strong conviction in order to go against the entire, nearly 2,000-year history of Christianity.[29]

Especially in the case of A. K. Emmerich, the emergence of this form in her visions is quite understandable when taking account of her childhood experiences. For this Y-form of the Cross with Christ hanging upon it was erected in almost life-like proportions in the Coesfeld Church near her birthplace and home, where she likely experienced the religious service most frequently. This statue probably impressed the young girl deeply and therefore entered her later visions so powerfully. That this Y-form corresponds not to the Cross on Golgotha but to the World-Tree in the etheric world, I have verified in my book *Und die Erde wird zur Sonne. Zum Mysterium der Auferstehung* [And the Earth Will Become a Sun. On the Mystery of the Resurrection].[30]

*Rudolf Steiner's pastel sketch from 1915 for the central motif of
the painting in the small cupola of the first Goetheanum. Detail.*
© Goetheanum Art Collection

To this untrue form of the Cross on Golgotha, J. v. Halle adds still one more detail that should not remain unmentioned here. In the final part of an essay in which she again takes up this theme, she writes: 'In a drastic manner, the Y-form of the Execution-mark [Cross] reveals within itself the destructive sign of the Anti-Christ.'[31] With regard to Golgotha, this 'Y-form' as 'sign of the Anti-Christ' exists neither on the physical plane nor on the etheric level. Therefore, one must ask oneself why the motif of Sorath is presented without further explanation – or rather, at this point the question should arise: What kind of beings in the spiritual world could they be who conjure up such images?

That the Y-form of the Cross on Golgotha is false and contradicts Rudolf Steiner's representations is clear from his many paintings, sketches and drafts dedicated to this theme. Especially in the pastel sketch for the central motif of the small cupola in the first Goetheanum, the middle Cross on the Golgotha Hill is unmistakably depicted in classical form. And one can assume that this drawing relates to the events on the physical plane, because the depiction shows the three crosses with a dark, almost black background; this scene is described in the Synoptic Gospels with the following words: 'From the sixth hour until the ninth, darkness spread over the whole land' (Matthew 27:45).[32]

*

Another contradiction to the Gospels and the tradition of the whole of Christianity is that according to J. v. Halle (and here she again follows A. K. Emmerich) the Baptism of Jesus did not take place in the Jordan River, but in a special baptismal font on a magical island, which had appeared out of nowhere for this purpose in the middle of the river.

J. v. Halle writes in an essay about the Baptism in the Jordan: 'The universe holds its breath for a moment of time, and out of the water of the river, into which John had just entered in order to prepare for the Baptism of the Lord, there arises, encompassed by the light and wind of the revelation of heavenly hosts, an island – such that the water parts and flows around the island. The island is only entered by the Baptist and the Higher Being to be baptized.'[33]

A. K. Emmerich also described the same pure wonder of the temporary emergence of an island out of the water of the Jordan River. However, as is often the case within her reports, the scene is far more specific and embellished with numerous greater and smaller details. According to her representation, the island did not appear immediately before the Baptism of Jesus, but even some time earlier. Before this, John and his pupils had prepared it beautifully with great effort and care. The point at issue here is that John and his pupils prepared this island in the middle of winter, and in a short time there emerged a flourishing summer landscape. She describes it as follows: 'John and his disciples planted twelve trees around the island; they were alive and they intertwined into an open arbour. I saw that John with his disciples planted smaller bushes between the trees, of which many were growing alongside the Jordan. They had white and red flowers, and yellow fruit with a little crown like medlars. It appeared very beautiful, for some were blooming and others were full of fruit.'[34]

This touching description does not arise from A. K. Emmerich's imagination, but is reflected from a supersensible reality that the visionary was not able to interpret correctly. This actually has to do with the emergence of a special ether-sphere at the baptismal site and encompassing its entire surroundings. For the etheric world of the Earth sprouts and buds with jubilant enthusiasm towards the Sun God, Who through His uniting with the Earth will become its new Spirit. The description of the blooming trees, hedges, flowers and fruit is the sensory image of this transformed etheric world.

So one can say: A. K. Emmerich perceived these events correctly, but interpreted them incorrectly, because she took the purely etheric processes to be physical-sensory in nature. J. v. Halle, by contrast, has seen the same event not only incorrectly, but has also not rightly understood it.

Rudolf Steiner, however, always spoke – connecting himself with the general Christian tradition, which he here, as in many other instances, found to be confirmed through his spiritual research – about the Baptism in the Jordan and not about an event on a magical island.[35]

An additional testimony to this is the whole iconography of this scene, which traces back to those individuals who from the fourth to tenth centuries, bore within themselves a replica of the etheric body of Jesus (from which various artists received their inspiration). Rudolf Steiner said in this regard: 'That was the reason why there could arise in them the great visions and archetypal ideas, which were then elaborated and given form by the great painters and sculptors' (GA 109, 11 April 1909).[36]

*

J. v. Halle completely disregards Rudolf Steiner's indication that Christ used a simple jasper chalice, although he clearly describes what actually took place: 'The sacred jasper cup of the Grail, which Christ made use of as He broke the bread, was used by Joseph of Arimathea to catch the blood from the wounds of Jesus' (GA 26, essay of January 1925).[37]

In contrast, J. v. Halle puts forward a very different picture,[38] which however does not differ greatly from A. K. Emmerich's description. According to A. K. Emmerich, the communion chalice was a very complicated apparatus, consisting of a double chalice (containing a pear-shaped vessel within it) surrounded by seven small cups mounted on a tray, with a pullout board, a little spoon stored in a leg of the chalice, and so forth.[39]

But one of the details given by J. v. Halle is new in comparison to her predecessor's description. She 'reveals' the secret of the material from which the chalice was made. It was 'living matter', which according to one of her descriptions, came from the Old Moon stage of evolution. (See *Das Abendmahl*, op. cit., p. 43.) However, according to spiritual science, this claim cannot be correct, because after the great Pralaya between the incarnations of Old Moon and the Earth there was not a single particle of the original Moon-material to be found on Earth.

If it were indeed as J. v. Halle claims, then according to Rudolf Steiner, this would have something to do with the Mystery of the Eighth Sphere or the sphere of evil. For the powers at the disposal of the adversaries enable Lucifer to form imaginations stemming from Old Moon, which Ahriman then fills with earthly matter. This results in something that can be perceived by physical eyes, yet has a very eerie character. This is therefore no *living* matter, but an actual creation of the opposing powers.

Rudolf Steiner describes this process as follows: 'Mark this well: instead of pure Imaginations being there, the imaginations are densified by the infusion of a mineral element that has been wrested from the Earth [by opposing powers]. In this way they are compressed, and densified imaginations are thus created. Thus we are enclosed in a world of *densified imaginations*, which are not

Moon imaginations for the simple reason that they are densified by the material element belonging to the Earth. They are spectres; that is to say, behind our world there is a world of spectres created by Lucifer and Ahriman' (GA 254, 18 October 1915, italics added). Now this spectral world is characterized by the fact that within it, imaginations that are otherwise experienced only outside the body and thus beyond all sense impressions, can now likewise be perceived with bodily senses.

And when in another description, J. v. Halle brings the material of the communion chalice into connection with the fifth layer of the Earth[40] – whereby she also contradicts herself[41] – this confirms the proximity of this material to the Ahrimanic region of the underworld. For according to Rudolf Steiner, Ahriman's permanent residence is in the sixth layer of the Earth's interior.[42]

Furthermore, according to Rudolf Steiner's characterization, this fifth layer – which he also calls the 'fruit Earth' – consists of a substance that is filled with powerful 'abounding growth energy', so that its destructive force can only be dispelled by the four strata above. 'Every little part of this [substance] grows out at once like sponge; it grows larger and larger and is held in place only by the upper layers' (GA 95, 4 September 1906). Hence, the idea under consideration is highly problematic, because from this substance a solid object is supposed to have been created on the Earth's surface, and to have remained intact for several centuries. To his description of the fifth layer, Rudolf Steiner adds: 'Here life is not restricted by form' (GA 94, 11 July 1906).

It should be noted that, based on an occult tradition, Rudolf Steiner indicates clearly the origin of the substance out of which the communion vessel was created in its simple chalice-form. It is related to the stone that dropped to Earth out of

Lucifer's crown when he fell. In summarizing this tradition, Rudolf Steiner states: 'Humanity possesses a deep secret, a Mystery, which holds sway in the world' (GA 92, 2 December 1907). Then follows the story of the communion chalice: 'When at the beginning of our evolution Lucifer fell from the ranks of those Spirits who guide humanity, a precious stone dropped from his crown, and out of this a chalice was formed. This same cup from which Christ Jesus drank with His disciples at the Last Supper, and this same cup in which the Blood that flowed on Golgotha was received by Joseph of Arimathea; this, Joseph of Arimathea brought to the West' (ibid.).

Here it is clearly stated that the origin of the substance out of which the communion chalice was formed lies in *spiritual heights* – namely, where before his fall Lucifer could legitimately reign – and is not to be found in the dark depths of the Earth's interior. Here, too, J. v. Halle delivers an image which leads in a direction opposite to that which one can find in Rudolf Steiner's descriptions.

*

Another example of an incorrect account can be found in relation to the Gethsemane scene, which A. K. Emmerich and J. v. Halle describe in a manner quite similar to one another. According to their presentations, it is imposed upon Christ Jesus that He must also answer for the *personal* mistakes, sins and omissions of all people; that is, He must take upon Himself all sins of each individual person.

In order to lend the appropriate drama to this thought, J. v. Halle even directly includes the readers of her book (that is, the former listeners of her presentation). This is what she says: 'Lucifer shows Him the enormity of the sins of mankind in the past, present and future. The dimension is indescribable. Take for example just your own "sin account", which is certainly not all too large, but already here one experiences a bad, oppresive feeling. Even these personal accounts, which we each carry with us and allow to grow throughout the course of our lives – even these Jesus Christ had to feel in his astral body during these hours [in Gethsemane]. Thus, *our* burdens were also imposed on Him. Let us just think of how much we must work to overcome for one life in the life after death. How immense must it be to carry, to bear the burdens of all human life?! A million times, a billion times more difficult' (*Und wäre Er nicht auferstanden...*, p. 129 G [p. 110 E], italics J. v. Halle).[43]

This point of view corresponds to the popular belief of the Catholic and other Christian churches; however in the Gospel of John, from the mouth of John the Baptist, it is testified: 'See, the Lamb of God, Who takes the sin *of the world* upon Himself' (John 1:29, italics added). These words hint at the Mystery that through His sacrifice on Golgotha, Christ did not take upon Himself the personal sins of humanity, which in the course of evolution must be balanced by the law of karma, but rather the objective consequences of human error for the whole further evolution of the Earth and the cosmos ('of the world').

Rudolf Steiner addressed this theme in a wonderful way in his lecture of 15 July 1914 (GA 155). According to his presentation, in order to be able to reconcile the law of karma with the idea of salvation, one must separate clearly the personal karma of a human being from the objective consequences of it that emerge for world evolution.

For a person will without doubt wish to balance out, in the course of his incarnations, the karma pertaining exclusively ·ŋ himself. When, at the latest after death, through true self-knowledge and in the light of world justice (and life in Kamaloka actually consists of this), a person gradually becomes aware of how he has made himself ever more imperfect through his bad deeds and all of his impure thoughts and emotions – and with this, what pain and suffering he caused to other people and even to higher beings – he will then strive for nothing else than to achieve the earliest possible balancing of these deeds in the course of his further incarnations. Christ, Who accompanies the human soul after death, will strengthen within the soul this desire to make good his errors in the future. In this situation, with respect to the person striving to justly compensate his own bad deeds, to take this opportunity away from him would amount to a cruelty of world guidance. However, through the law of karma and reincarnation this opportunity is afforded him in full.

This gives expression to the fact that when a person has reached the end of Earth evolution, he will have managed to make good his personal karma. However, the objective damage that he inflicted upon the world through all of his bad deeds – and which, since having been carried out, exist objectively in the world – cannot be compensated for in this manner. For this task, a person needs the help of Christ, who in this higher sense takes precisely 'the sins of the world' upon Himself. If Christ had not brought the sacrifice of connecting Himself with the *objective consequences* of human karma, then mankind could never achieve the true goal of its development – and with this, nor could the Earth.

Rudolf Steiner brings this Christ-law to expression in the following statement: 'The stain that we have personally contracted is adjusted in our karma, but the objective fact remains – we cannot efface that by removing our own imperfection. We must discriminate between the consequences of a sin for ourselves, and the consequences of a sin for the objective course of the world. It is highly important that we should make this distinction' (GA 155, 15 July 1914).

A little later, when he returns to the problem of the 'forgiveness of sins', Rudolf Steiner expresses this fact in the same lecture even more decidedly: 'For the saying, "Your sins are forgiven", denotes a *cosmic fact* and *not a karmic fact*' (ibid., italics Rudolf Steiner). Therein lies the fundamental difference: The fact that Christ took upon Himself the objective consequences of mankind's sins is not a *karmic*, but a *cosmic* deed! And the dimension of this is undoubtedly infinitely greater than the sum of all individual human errors and sins.

Of course, this question is treated entirely differently in the Catholic Church, where the dogma allows no knowledge of reincarnation and karma; the forgiveness of sins through Christ is seen to relate only to the misdemeanours of individual people. Moreover, the Church positions itself as mediator between Christ and the human being. On the basis of this position, as an earthly institution, it exerts an influence upon the human conscience and not infrequently even makes demands of it; thus, it is able to greatly increase its power over the souls of believers. Indeed, the Church believes that it alone can forgive people their sins in the name of Christ.

However, Christ says: 'You must not think that I have come to abolish the Law or the Prophets. My task is not to abolish but to fulfil' (Matthew 5:17). And the greatest law of justice is precisely that of karma, which each person who aspires for wholeness will wish to follow. Therefore, to the statement just quoted, Christ immediately adds the following words, which clearly indicate the full dimension of the karmic law (for the Law of Moses does not contain such a dimension): 'Yes, I say to you: Until Heaven and Earth pass away, not a letter, not a jot or tittle of the Law shall lose its validity. Everything must first be fulfilled' (5:18).

Therefore, Christ ensures that the law of karma remains valid for every individual; for this reason He only takes upon Himself the objective consequences of sin for the Earth and the cosmos, so that in this way the whole of our future evolution through Jupiter, Venus and Vulcan may at all be possible.

At this point one can say: With respect to this topic, when A. K. Emmerich represents the entire event out of her visions incorrectly, then one can at least understand why this is so. As a child, she was raised a strict Catholic and was deeply associated with the Catholic Church and its teachings, knowing nothing about karma and reincarnation – not to mention having an understanding of these matters from an anthroposophical point of view. Therefore, she could not perceive the difference between personal and objective karma, which, as we have just seen above, in each case must be balanced differently.

J. v. Halle, on the other hand, should certainly know these foundational anthroposophical truths. Therefore, it is beyond comprehension why she would simply repeat A. K. Emmerich's error, which contradicts everything Rudolf Steiner had to say about this. One can only clarify this by recognizing that she does not wish to proceed in accordance with Rudolf Steiner and his spiritual research, but – as in many other instances – places her own sensory visions or 'time-journeys' above Rudolf Steiner's research and insights.

*

A further detail in connection with the Gethsemane scene must still be mentioned here. J. v. Halle describes one of her visions, in which is revealed to her the ascent of the Jahve deity from the Moon to the Sun. This would mean, however, that as of the time of the event in Gethsemane, Jahve was no longer connected with the Moon, but rather from that time on – as he was originally, being one of the seven Sun Elohim – was once again to be found on the Sun. Or in J. v. Halle's words: 'It was as though the Jahve deity was released from his darkness, his indirect luminous quality, and in the moment of the affirmed sacrifice of the Logos [this refers to Christ in Gethsemane], he [Jahve] left newly radiating from the Moon to the spiritual Sun' (*Und wäre Er nicht auferstanden...*, p. 132 G [pp. 113-114 E]).[44]

This claim, however, contradicts the fact that Jahve continues to remain connected with the Moon even in our time; for his task consists precisely in resisting, from the Moon, the absorbing tendency of the Eighth Sphere until the time when the Earth – together with the humanity connected with it – have become so advanced they can endure the reuniting with the Moon. Only then will Jahve's cosmic mission on the Moon be complete; and at that point he can once again ascend to the Sun. Rudolf Steiner says in this regard: 'Jahve or Jehovah, then, must be regarded as that Being who even in the physical domain has ensured that not all materiality can be drawn away by Lucifer and Ahriman [into the Eighth Sphere]. And then, at the right time, equal care will be taken by the same Spirit [Jehova] that the Moon shall re-enter the Earth when the Earth is strong enough to receive it, when the danger is overcome through the development that will have meanwhile taken place' (GA 254, 18 October 1915).

That Jahve had separated himself much earlier from the earthly destiny of the Hebrew people, Jesus of Nazareth had come to experience prior to the Baptism in the Jordan, when, through his many-years' occupation with Jewish spirituality, he ascertained that the Bath Kol, which had previously inspired the prophets as a spiritual voice, was no longer active amongst his people. But Bath Kol had been the Being who mediated between the Moon-deity Jahve and the Hebrew people whom Jahve guided.

*

A further example is another of those that one is really reluctant to go into. Both authors provide a gruesome description of how the Hierarchies (J. v. Halle calls them 'entities'; for A. K. Emmerich they are angels) move through the streets of Jerusalem and collect everywhere 'scraps' of the Redeemer's physical body, which were torn from the body during His martyrdom, as well as all drops of blood and sweat that He had shed, in order to reinsert them in the corresponding places of the injured body.

J. v. Halle's reasoning for why this was necessary is that without this missing material, Christ's body – this means as purely material body – could not be Resurrected completely intact. 'Many entities came to all the places of the passion and collected in an occult, alchemical process the shreds of skin and flesh, blood and sweat from Jesus' body, which were separated through the tortures, the fall and his fears, and integrated these substances into the earthly body [German: 'Erdenleib']. ... It was a real labour of the Hierarchies to assemble everything in the proper manner in order to make the new Earth "complete" ' (*Und wäre Er nicht auferstanden...*, p. 160 G [pp. 138-139 E]).[45]

Although it is obvious that in writing her books J. v. Halle occupied herself with the cycle *From Jesus to Christ*, it seems she cannot understand the most important insight described in it, namely the fundamental difference between the

59

Phantom as 'spirit-body' (GA 131, 12 October 1911), and the matter that fills it. For these two elements take quite different paths after Christ Jesus' death on Golgotha. The Phantom descends into the interior of the Earth while the material components of the body, which break down into the finest dust, are received by the fissure in the Earth.[46] However, there is no place in the descriptions of A. K. Emmerich and J. v. Halle for what really happened, and about which we learn through Rudolf Steiner's spiritual research.[47] For their visions have nothing to do with modern spiritual research and lead (it would be more correct to say: lead astray) in a quite different direction.

The only situation in which the physical body of Christ Jesus could actually have been damaged in its form was the moment when the soldiers wanted to break the legs of the Crucified One. This, however, was not allowed to happen. Not because the Phantom would have been adversely affected (in any case, as spiritual being it would have remained unscathed, above and beyond the fact that it was already separate from the matter of the physical body[48]), but for a yet entirely different reason.

Here we are concerned with the fact that of all people on Earth, Christ was the first and only to have brought completely under the power of His 'I' during His earthly life the densest mineral component of the human body, the bone-system. Rudolf Steiner reports about this: 'Never before had there been in all of Earth evolution up until the Baptism of Christ Jesus by John – neither among initiated nor uninitiated people – a human Individuality who had power even over the chemical and physical processes of the bone-system. Through Christ's entry into the body of Jesus of Nazareth, the presence of the Christ-'I' became master of the bone system. The consequence was that for once on Earth there lived a body that was able to gain mastery of its powers to such an extent that it could incorporate the shape of the bone-system, the spiritual form of the bone-system, into Earth evolution' (GA 112, 3 July 1909).

And in another lecture Rudolf Steiner added to this fact the following: 'This indicates to us that through this mastery of the bones [through Christ in Jesus], a force entered the world which was indeed able to conquer death in physical matter; for the bones [as mineral component of the physical body] are to blame for the fact that humanity experiences death' (GA 105, 14 August 1908). Now, however, through the indwelling power of the Son of God, the bones were thereby prepared and made ready to disintegrate into the finest dust in the grave, in order then within the Earth to go the appropriate ways.[49] It is for this reason that human beings were not allowed to interfere wilfully in this process.[50]

From all that has been said, it is clear why it was necessary for the bone-structure of Jesus' body to remain intact even after His death. John, who knew this Mystery well, describes the incident in his Gospel. He reports: 'When they came to Jesus and saw that He had already died, they did not break His legs ... All this happened so that the scripture should be fulfilled: His bones shall not be broken' (John 19:33 and 36). Thus it is expressed that especially the bone-system of Jesus' body should remain, even after His death, solely under the guidance of the divine force of that Being Who had previously dwelt within Him.

Thus Rudolf Steiner's spiritual research shows, in this case as well, a very different picture of the events than that mediated through the visions which J. v. Halle, faithfully following A. K. Emmerich, offers to the reader.

In addition, what has been said testifies to the fact that not only Christ Jesus, but also both robbers were *crucified* (i.e. hammered with nails onto the wood). Whether they were additionally tied with a rope to the beams will be left open here as being of less importance.

Likewise in this matter, J. v. Halle represents a completely different perspective, and allows herself to be guided solely by her own visions without questioning their veracity. She describes, namely, that the two robbers – in contrast to Christ Jesus – were not nailed to the wood, but only tied with ropes to T-shaped crosses, and in such a way that they could support themselves with their arms on the cross beams.[51] However, this claim is not true.

As described in the Gospel of John, all three crucified persons were to have had their legs broken for the following reason: 'Since it was the Day of Preparation, the Jews did not want the bodies to remain on the Cross, for that Sabbath was a great festival day. So they asked Pilate that their legs might be broken and that they should be taken down from the Cross' (John 19:31). This conveys that due to the holiness of the dawning Sabbath day, the death of the three crucified persons should be accelerated so that they could be removed from the crosses before evening.

When the soldiers returned to the Golgotha Hill, they found that one of those crucified had already died. Thus, it was only necessary to break the legs of the two robbers who were still alive. The reason for this brutal action was that the crucified men were able to support themselves on their intact legs in order to catch their breath. However, when this possibility was denied by breaking the leg bones, they died very quickly from suffocation. If the two robbers had not been nailed to the cross, but only tied onto it, and indeed with arms laid over the cross beams, as J. v. Halle describes it (and as it is also incorrectly illustrated in a few works of art, contrary to the Gospel of John), then they still would have lived for hours even with broken legs, and the endeavour pursued by the Jews would not have been achieved.

*

Another example of how J. v. Halle's presentations blatantly contradict Rudolf Steiner's statements will be cited here. First, she describes Christ leaving the grave almost exactly as one can read in the accounts of A. K. Emmerich and T. Neumann.[52] Then she further adds the following incident: 'Now I must report about an event that a person who thinks purely materialistically would have to consider impossible: In that Christ's spirit-body ascends out of the grave, the physical-material shroud will be forever stripped off, in a physical and supersensible way. It arises as if borne on the wind, floats with the ascending Christ – I stress explicitly: the fabric of the cloth passes through the substance of the rock that forms the burial grave – and falls rolled up back into the grave niche after Christ's ascension is completed. There it remains lying, just like the face cloth' (*Und wäre Er nicht aufer-standen...*, p. 152 G [pp. 131-132 E]).[53]

By the obvious emphases that J. v. Halle uses in describing this scene, the attention of the reader is primarily directed to the shroud, which miraculously passes through the material of the rock and then – once again travelling through the rock – falls back into the grave, to remain lying there in the way it is later found by the disciples.

Now let us compare this description with that given by Rudolf Steiner, to whom this seemingly small detail of the account of the shroud – however, for entirely different reasons – is also very important. In the lectures about the Fifth Gospel, he reports from his spiritual research: 'The consideration from the Fifth Gospel shows – this is one of the great impressions that one can gain when one investigates what is given in the Fifth Gospel – that after Christ Jesus' body had been laid in the grave, something really occurred whereby finally things could be as the Gospel of John so wonderfully describes: how the grave is empty and how the cloths lay all around. This is how it was. This is what the Fifth Gospel shows us. It was like this, because a wave-like earthquake had taken place and caused a fissure in the Earth. The body of Christ Jesus fell into this fissure. Then the fissure closed up again. Due to the wave-like movements and storms,[54] the shrouds were actually strewn around and found in the position described in the Gospel of John when the condition of the empty tomb is depicted [John 20:5-7]. This is a great, heart-warming impression when one discovers these things through the Fifth Gospel and then finds them confirmed in the Gospel of John' (GA 148, 10 February 1914).

In becoming aware of this description, the question immediately arises as to why Rudolf Steiner, during his spiritual research, was so impressed by this seemingly small detail – the arrangement of the shrouds in the grave as a result of the earth-quake and strong 'whirlwind'. For only two years before this, he expressed in the following words how moved he had been during his spiritual research of this scene: 'It was astonishing to me, after I had discovered from occult research that an earthquake had occurred, to find it pointed to in the Gospel of Matthew. The Earth split, the dust of the corpse fell in and merged with the whole substance of the Earth. Due to the vibrations caused by the earthquake, the cloths were shaken up just as one can find it described in the narration of the John Gospel. Thus, we can grasp the Resurrection in an occult manner and do not need to contra-dict the Gospels' (GA 130, 9 February 1912).

The reason for Rudolf Steiner's strong reaction while researching *this* fact seems to me to lie in the realization that for the first time in human history, it was possible for an initiate to bring down to Earth and to describe, from the high regions of the spiritual world – where the true Akashic Record originates – such a small detail as the story of the shroud, which he had previously been able to research with great accuracy: and then to find this fact fully confirmed in another source, the Gospel of John. (In further lectures about the Fifth Gospel, Rudolf Steiner also speaks in a similar manner regarding the earthquake and the solar eclipse.)

Here one should clearly consider what it really means for the further evolution of humanity that through modern Christian initiation, it is actually possible to research the Akashic Record with such precision and objectivity as one otherwise knows only in natural-scientific contexts! Moreover, one should bear in mind that specific details from the life of Christ Jesus on Earth are much more difficult for true spiritual research to decipher in the Akashic Record than is a general overview of the development of the Earth or the cosmos. Therefore, for a true spiritual researcher it is infinitely more complicated to investigate in the spiritual world such a seemingly small thing like the position of the shrouds in the grave chamber than to survey great cosmic cycles and periods.

In the following shattering words, Rudolf Steiner gave expression to what is required by such research in the Akashic Record about details of Christ Jesus's life: 'What has just been said may sound grotesque, but it is nevertheless true that one cannot research such matters as those pertaining to the life of Jesus of Nazareth unless the words "One is consumed to serve the Spirits of Personality as spiritual food" have real meaning for one. [...] "I am food for the Archai, I am digested by the Archai, this is their life, which I live in them" – to experience this means placing oneself into the consciousness of the Spirits of Personality, the Archai' (GA 148, 18 December 1913).

This means, however, that only out of the intrinsic connection with the consciousness of elevated Hierarchical beings at the stage of Time Spirits, can one research within the spiritual world such matters as the details in Christ Jesus' life on Earth. And that one can discover from out of this source how the shrouds were arranged in the grave, as well as the nature of what caused this (namely, an earthquake and the whirlwind) – precisely this is what had so deeply impressed Rudolf Steiner in this instance.

With this story of the shrouds, Rudolf Steiner asks us to pay attention to two things. First, to the new possibilities and extraordinary precision of modern spiritual research; and second, to the fact that there was nothing magical on any level with regard to all the events that took place during the Mystery of Golgotha and its surroundings. Everything related to the aspect of the Son of Man was entirely human; and everything concerning the aspect of the Son of God was fully and entirely cosmic.[55] These events had nothing at all to do with magic – which was, on the other hand, represented by the great magician and initiate Apollonius of Tyana, a contemporary of Christ Jesus.[56]

Therefore, the assertion does not belong in this context that the shrouds, as material objects in the physical-sense world, could raise themselves through the material substance of a stone and then once more fall back through the stone, in order finally to lie as it is described in the Gospel. Nothing magical is associated with the entirety of the events surrounding the death and Resurrection on Golgotha. All manner of magical things can be brought into relation to the activity of Apollonius and similar figures; not, however, to the life of Christ Jesus.[57]

Yet in J. v. Halle's publications, there is ever and again the tendency to introduce something entirely magical into Christ Jesus' earthly life. In this regard, she does not even hold off before the Resurrection event. She writes in her book *Der Abstieg in die Erdenschichten*, Dornach 2008 [In English: *The Descent into the Layers of the Earth*. Temple Lodge 2011]: 'The Anti-Christ connected himself to the Christ Spirit, Who made His way to the centre of the Earth. He moved with Christ down to the ninth layer, in the direction of the Earth's centre. ... Sorath's final plan was to further take part in the Resurrection – in an "attached" way, to misuse the Christian deed – and thus to thwart its impulse forever' (p. 114 G [p. 107 E]). The notion that Sorath could have 'connected' to Christ on His way to the Resurrection in an '"attached" way' pertains, in my view, to a very serious lack of understanding on the part of J. v. Halle regarding the essential nature of the Resurrection. At this point, the reader must at least really attempt to imagine how such a 'taking part' could possibly have occured.

The above-quoted assertion by J. v. Halle is thus not only unacceptable because she contradicts Rudolf Steiner's spiritual research, but also for the reason that such stories once again bring a magical element into connection with an occurrence to which such an element is fundamentally alien.[58] For a direct attack by Sorath (with a real possibility of success) would only have been possible if Christ Himself had in some way applied magical means. However, this could only have happened on Earth; that is, during the three years following the Baptism in the Jordan.

Rudolf Steiner speaks about this quite clearly in one place in his lecture cycle on the Apocalypse: 'This being [Sorath] could only have taken hold of something from the Earth if at a certain moment he could have gained mastery, namely *where the Christ principle descended to the Earth.* If this Christ principle had been suffocated at its starting point, if Christ had been overcome by the adversary, then certainly it would have been possible for the whole Earth to succumb to the Sorath principle' (GA 104, 30 June 1908, italics added).

However, because during His three-year life Christ engaged in absolutely no magical acts – and moreover fundamentally ruled out everything magical – there was no point of attack given,[59] on the basis of which Sorath could have combated Him with a hope of success.

Above all, however, Sorath simply had nothing to do with the event of the Resurrection, because it took place in the exalted and sublime sphere to which no evil power, not even the Sun Demon, could have gained access. And if someone brings the influence of Sorath into connection with the Resurrection, he only thereby demonstrates that he has not yet comprehended the greatness of this event.

*

J. v. Halle's peculiar notion about the relation of the Phantom to the matter that penetrates it is perhaps most clearly expressed in another of her publications. There she claims – with regard to the raising of Lazarus – that John, son of Zebedee sacrificed his own etheric body to Lazarus, and that following this, John Zebedee's material body was instantly disintegrated to dust: '…in this way John, son of Zebedee's physical being disappeared from the Earth, for he gave up his physical body in order to sacrifice his etheric body to the new disciple [Lazarus-John], who would there come into being. … This etheric body endowed to the new disciple could then build up for itself a new physical body within a short amount of time' (*Das Mysterium des Lazarus...*, p. 123).[60]

About this wondrous emergence of a new physical body virtually out of nothing, J. v. Halle writes further: 'And at the very least, in this case – at the moment of awakening and in the following hours – this etheric body [of Zebedee], guided from above by its higher members, builds up for itself the appropriate physical body [for Lazarus-John]' (ibid., p. 124). And then she adds that this construction of a new physical body for Lazarus-John 'came about with extraordinary speed, but even so, took a few hours' (ibid., p. 125).

Apart from the fact that this process appears altogether quite magical, it is in principle impossible. A body can only disintegrate into dust *immediately* if its material component, yet while the human being is still alive, is separated from the Phantom; and this separation can only occur if the Phantom has been completely restored – a process which within the whole of humanity had come to pass only in the case of Christ Jesus, Who required *three years* for this restoration process. With regard to all other human beings (including the highest initiates, to the ranks of which one cannot count John, son of Zebedee[61]), even if they die in such a way that the etheric body quickly withdraws,[62] the physical form of the body is initially retained, until it gradually dissolves into the elements of the Earth.[63]

Thus, everything that happened with the body of Jesus of Nazareth is unique and also very complicated. For in order actually to become dust in the grave, this body still needed, in addition to the three-year work of the Christ Spirit indwelling it, the additional treatment of spices mentioned in the Gospel: 'Nicodemus came also, who had first come to Jesus in the realm of night, and he brought roughly one hundred pounds of a mixture of myrrh and aloes. And they took the body of Jesus and wrapped it in strips of linen soaked with the balsam spices, according to the burial custom of the Jews' (John 19:39-40).

Only through this process could the body disintegrate to dust in a relatively short time, as Rudolf Steiner describes: 'You must not suppose that this body in which the Christ dwelt – let us say a year-and-a-half after the Baptism by John in the Jordan – was like any other body. Rather, it was in such a state that an ordinary human soul would have felt at once that it was falling away from him, because it could only be held together by the powerful macrocosmic Christ Being. It was a slow and gradual dying process that continued for three years. And this body had reached the verge of dissolution when the Mystery of Golgotha took place. Then it was only necessary that those people mentioned in the narrative should come to the body with their unusual preparations, which are referred to as spices, and bring about a chemical union between these special substances and the body of Jesus of Nazareth, in which the macrocosmic Christ Being had dwelt for three years; and subsequently, that they should place this body in the grave. In this condition, very little was needed before this body dissolved to dust in the grave' (GA 130, 9 January 1912).

All this was possible only because Christ had previously fully restored the Phantom of Jesus of Nazareth's physical body in an internal alchemical process, which finally came to completion on Good Friday upon the Golgotha Hill. 'By the point at which this body of Jesus of Nazareth was nailed to the Cross, the Phantom was indeed fully intact, existing as spirit-body – though only in supersensibly visible form' (GA 131, 12 October 1911). This shows that at the time of the Raising of Lazarus, the process concerned had not yet come to an end for Christ. If the disintegration-to-dust of John Zebedee's body – together with the emergence of a new body for Lazarus-John – had actually been possible out of nothing, so to speak, then the Mystery of Golgotha would no longer have needed to take place.

Despite everything outlined here, J. v. Halle claims to have seen these events with her 'sensory eyes', and describes this as follows: '*For the sensory eyes*, the situation is such that through Christ's calling forth of Lazarus, the physical-material body of John Zebedee vanished within a few moments, collapsing into dust' (*Das Mysterium des Lazarus...*, p. 136, italics added). The process of transforming the matter of the physical body to dust – which is only possible through a complete restoration of the Phantom – had in the case of Christ required three years of His earthly life. For John, son of Zebedee, however, who was not even an initiate, this process is supposed to have happened quite simply and without any effort,[64] and merely on account of his etheric body having so suddenly left the physical body.

Despite the absurdity of this whole story, J. v. Halle adamantly claims that she saw it all herself: 'For I myself have perceived this transformation of Lazarus into the disciple whom the Lord loved, not only as a spiritual but also as a sensory-physical fact that had come about at that time …' (ibid., p. 148).

In this regard, every attentive reader would have to ask the author the question: What actually happened with Lazarus' old body, which, according to all of the fantastic events described by J. v. Halle still lay in the grave – and which after the stone was rolled away, was still to be seen by the group of people standing in front of the grave? For as we have already learned, according to J. v. Halle there had been created for Lazarus-John – with the help of Zebedee – an entirely new body, which had nothing to do with his old body. Thus, given that Lazarus suddenly appeared in a new physical body – whose facial features resembled those of John, son of Zebedee rather than Lazarus – the many people from the village of Bethany who witnessed all of these transformations would have had to ask to whom the body still lying in the grave actually belonged. J. v. Halle says: 'In that the etheric body of John, son of Zebedee was transferred to Lazarus, this etheric body was able to build up for him – under the direction of the higher spiritual members – a new physical body, which essentially bore John Zebedee's characteristics' (ibid., p. 82). Thereby, J. v. Halle once more testifies to her conviction that Lazarus received a new physical body from John Zebedee, while his original physical body simply lay in the grave for everyone to see. Unfortunately, the author does not provide a clarification about this in her book.

At this point at the very latest, one should realize just how far J. v. Halle is going. For her fantastic description implies nothing less than that the Raising of Lazarus, as the Gospel of John reports it (and this description comes from the person who was not only a personal witness of this event, but to whom it actually happened), had never taken place! And, according to J. v. Halle, the Evangelist's following representation does not correspond to reality: 'Then they took away the stone. ... [And Jesus] called with a loud voice, "Lazarus, come forth!" And the dead man came out, his hands and feet bound with strips of linen, his face covered with a veil. And Jesus said, "Unbind him, and let him go!"' (John 11:41 and 11:43-44). Yet J. v. Halle says that the bound body remained in the grave and a whole new body for Lazarus' 'I' was created within a few hours (where exactly?) – a body, however, which bore John Zebedee's facial features, so that nobody could recognize him, not even his sisters their own brother.

The outrageous nature of this account of the events need not surprise us. For wherever it is a matter of J. v. Halle's sensory visions, she places them without hesitation above the Gospel accounts and the results of Rudolf Steiner's spiritual research. (Further examples of this can be found later in this chapter.) So in order to convince her listeners and readers of the accuracy of her visions, she makes the following statement in the Preface to her book: 'These remarks emerge from an independent spiritual experience and therefore contain no hypotheses nor speculations' (*Das Mysterium des Lazarus...*, p. 10).[65]

*

With regard to Lazarus' dead body, J. v. Halle reports the following strange incident, which is closely aligned to the account given by A. K. Emmerich. The latter claimed that after his death, Lazarus was initially laid out in his house for three or four days, before – following a further four days in the grave – the Raising was finally carried out. About this J. v. Halle writes: 'I have been made aware of the fact that in the descriptions of Anna Katharina Emmerich, one reads of seven or eight days passing between the time of death and the Raising' (ibid., p. 117).

To the apparent contradiction between A. K. Emmerich's opinion and the report in the Gospel ('When Jesus arrived, he found that he had already been in the tomb for four days', John 11:17) and probably also to justify the accuracy of her predecessor's visions and thus to place them above the report of the Gospel, J. v. Halle expresses the following: 'In addition, one can say that in accordance with the Jewish rites of the time, it was common in many houses to initially lay out the deceased in the house for the duration of three days' (*Das Mysterium des Lazarus...*, p. 118). Although in this case she affiliates herself closely with A. K. Emmerich, she adds further: 'Inasmuch as they [the sisters of Lazarus] knew nothing about *Christian* initiation,

73

it was clear to them that one could only finally place Lazarus in the grave *after* the period of those three days' (ibid., p. 119, italics J. v. Halle). Thus, she also arrives at seven days: three in the house and four in the grave.

She states all this, however, with the specific intention of proving through her own visions – supported by those of A. K. Emmerich – that the Raising of Lazarus was not an initiation in the original sense. For in such a situation, a death-like sleep lasted only *three-and-a-half* days.[66] (That is, the neophyte was Raised on the fourth day.) With J. v. Halle's description, however, it is a matter of a corpse that is already one week old and thus, especially considering the heat of the area, was already decaying. She herself says: 'Therefore, there can be no talk of a sleep-condition; not even of the three-day Mystery sleep common at that time, as conducted by the pre-Christian adepts' (ibid., p. 67). For, in her opinion, 'with Lazarus, the physical-material death had occurred' (ibid.).

In another passage from the same book, she reaffirms this thought once again: 'When the physical body of Lazarus had decomposed, and when with this, indeed, the etheric body had separated itself from it and dissolved ...' (ibid., p. 69), and further: 'then this part [the material body] of the old Lazarus had already gone over into the irreversible process of decomposition' (ibid., p. 78). In this way, J. v. Halle says that Lazarus' body could not be awakened to life after a week-long process of decay; this is why he needed a completely new body – which is supposed to have been provided by Zebedee's sacrifice – in order to go on living.

Thus, the author sets the Raising of Lazarus in clear contradiction to Rudolf Steiner's presentation of this. He consistently represented the point of view, first with the release of his early book *Christianity as Mystical Fact and the Mysteries of*

Antiquity (GA 8), and later through his Christological lecture cycles, that according to his spiritual research the Raising of Lazarus was a matter of a singular, publicly conducted *initiation* – which, as in all Mysteries, was preceded by a three-and-a-half-day sleep.[67] For Lazarus absolutely needed this unique initiation in order to become the only earthly person to stand fully consciously under the Cross on Golgotha.

Seen from a spiritual-scientific perspective, the story illustrated by J. v. Halle is simply impossible also for the following reason: No etheric body alone can produce a physical body on Earth – its task in human life consists only of supporting and enlivening the physical body. The creation of the physical body occurs – as far as its spiritual essence is concerned – through the 'I' of the person with the help of the Spiritual Hierarchies in upper Devachan, between death and a new birth. Such a creation of a physical body 'out of nothing' would only be possible from out of the spiritual forces of the Cosmic Midnight Hour, which Christ brought to Earth for the first time through His Resurrection.[68] Otherwise, such a deed would have had a purely magical character. And the Christ Being had nothing whatsoever to do with magic of any kind.

To achieve such a creation not through magic but in a cosmic way, is not possible for any initiate, regardless how advanced he is in his development. Only the fully restored Phantom of Christ Jesus had such power over earthly matter that this process could be accomplished. This amounted to the complete overcoming of death, which happened in an unparalleled way on the Golgotha Hill, and not in the grave at Bethany.

The only 'proof' that J. v. Halle cites in her book to support her construction (aside from the constant reference to her sensory visions) is a reference to John the Baptist, who according to Rudolf Steiner[69] possessed *in the spiritual world* after his death the forces of the higher members of the human being (Spirit-Self, Life-Spirit and Spirit-Man). J. v. Halle infers from this that precisely with the help of the forces of Spirit-Man, which John the Baptist possessed posthumously, it had become possible to create a new body for Lazarus-John *on Earth*. However, also in this attempt to bring her own visions into connection with anthroposophical ideas, she is entirely in error.

For after death, every person has a natural relation with his higher members. Moreover, for his 'I' they become new super-sensible sheaths in which the person lives on in the spiritual world, and can rise ever higher. Rudolf Steiner says in this regard: 'Just as a person here [on Earth] envelops himself in the astral, etheric and physical bodies, so when [after death] he grows into the spiritual world, does he enshroud himself in Spirit-Self, Life-Spirit and Spirit-Man' (GA 168, 18 February 1916). There they are not yet the person's possession, but a merciful gift of the higher Hierarchies. These spiritual members will only fully belong to the human 'I' in the coming evolutionary stages of Jupiter, Venus and Vulcan. Hence, they cannot be used in the manner that J. v. Halle imagines.

There is only one Being Who was in possession of and could fully control the forces of Spirit-Man *on Earth* in the sense of the Vulcan stage of our cosmos – that was Christ Jesus. (See Appendix 2 below.) No human being could perform upon Earth or from out of the spiritual world such a creation of a physical body from nothing, neither before nor after the Mystery of Golgotha.

There is yet something further pertaining to this. In order to create a physical body, the 'I' (not the etheric body) of the person concerned would also have to hold full power over the bone system. As already stated, only Christ among all people and initiates had such power over this element. Here J. v. Halle apparently confuses what only Christ as a divine Being can accomplish, with what she thinks is possible for a normal person, initiate or deceased person. And yet Christ did not perform such an action with regard to Lazarus, because it would not have corresponded to the legitimate development of Earth, and consequently would have amounted to nothing other than black magic.

At this point one really should imagine concretely how this whole account according to J. v. Halle could have taken place on the physical plane. Christ Jesus, accompanied by His disciples, by Mary and Martha and many people from the village, approaches the sealed grave. The stone is lifted away and in the grave one sees Lazarus' dead body wrapped in shrouds. Christ calls, 'Lazarus, come forth!' (John 11:43). The words 'come forth!' belong to a sacred Mystery formula that has been used for millennia within the Mysteries in relation to the initiation of mystics. However, a corpse cannot bring itself to movement. Furthermore, it can no longer be revived, for within the period of a week (as A. K. Emmerich and J. v. Halle have described it) the processes of disintegration would already have been too far advanced. What is said to have happened at that moment, however, is that the physical body of one of the twelve disciples, John the son of Zebedee, transformed itself, according to J. v. Halle, instantly into a little heap of dust; and this in the midst of a great crowd of people. At the same time, there somehow, somewhere arises out of nothing – and this process, according to J. v. Halle, lasts only a few hours – a new body as Lazarus, which has absolutely nothing to do with the body that continues to lie in the grave.

Thereby, Christ plays virtually no part in these two processes. For His words 'come forth!' pertain to *the body of Lazarus lying in the grave.* The disappearance of John Zebedee's physical body, however, would merely have been the result of the activity of his own 'I' (and completely intact Phantom) – which would have had to possess the power to draw the etheric body out of the physical body so quickly that the latter would disappear in an instant. Then, with the emergence of a new physical body for Lazarus, it would again have been primarily the same Zebedee acting from out of the spiritual world, who to this end would have contributed his etheric body. And to assist in this process, there would have come as well the 'I' of John the Baptist, enveloped in his Spirit-Man element in the spiritual world.

Again, according to this account, the following words of the Gospel do not apply: namely that Lazarus, 'his feet and hands bound with strips of linen, his face covered with a veil' (John 11:44), as he was prepared according to the Jewish burial rites by his sisters and friends, emerged from out of the grave. For according to J. v. Halle, Lazarus' corpse remained motionless in the grave; and the newly fashioned body of Lazarus surely would not have been created already wrapped in grave cloths and provided with a veil. Yet, in J. v. Halle's imagination apparently all this was possible through magical arts. Then, however, one would have to identify it as black magic.

It is entirely clear that these visions of J. v. Halle can be brought together neither with the description from the John Gospel, nor with the results of Rudolf Steiner's research. However, this does not concern her. Undeterred, she believes solely her own visions, and apparently places no value on the fact that it is the Raised Lazarus-John himself who reports on all these events in the John Gospel.

In this connection, it is of further significance to recall more exactly the story of the miraculous catch of fish from the last chapter of the John Gospel. From the content of this story, it once more becomes clear how seriously J. v. Halle contradicts the Evangelist. For in her book she claims that following the events previously described, the John Zebedee being – now consisting only of 'I' and astral body in the spiritual world – came into connection with the bodily sheaths of his brother James: 'Thus, after giving up his etheric and physical bodies, the soul-spiritual being of John the son of Zebedee incorporated itself into his brother James' (*Das Mysterium des Lazarus...*, p. 87).

As a result of this process after the Raising of Lazarus, with reference to *the physical plane* there would no longer have been two Zebedee brothers. Instead there would only have been one body, that of James, now inhabited by two 'I's: his own and that of his brother. In other words, from this moment on we would have to do with the physical presence no longer of two Johns, but only of one – namely, Lazarus-John.

The twenty-first chapter of the Gospel of John, however, begins with a statement by its author that clearly contradicts the above-mentioned assertion of J. v. Halle: 'Simon Peter, Thomas called the Twin, Nathanael from Cana in Galilee, *the sons of Zebedee* and two other of His disciples were together' (John 21:2, italics added). After the *two* sons of Zebedee are mentioned, the situation is further described in the seventh verse: 'Then the disciple whom Jesus loved said to Peter, "It is the Lord!"' In the twentieth verse, this sacred expression 'the disciple whom the Lord loved' is additionally used in connection with the Last Supper, during which John lay on the breast of the Lord. These Gospel-citations make clear that at the meal, which the Risen One prepared for His disciples on the shore following the fishing, there were *two* John-disciples present on the physical plane: Zebedee's sons – James and *John* – and *Lazarus-John.*

Of course, J. v. Halle is free to consider the reports of John in this passage null and void. However, precisely this statement in the Gospel is of particular importance, because it clearly verifies that Rudolf Steiner was correct when – contrary to the conventional Christian tradition, according to which John, son of Zebedee is thought to be the author of the fourth Gospel – he kept the two John-figures apart, in order to bear witness from out of his spiritual research to the truth that John, son of Zebedee continued to live on physically even after Christ's Resurrection (as did his brother James), and along with them, or 'the disciple whom the Lord loved' – however, as a different discrete individuality.

Like all other examples – and the number of these instances could be still significantly increased from out of J. v. Halle's books[70] – this example shows that the author wishes to follow only her visions, in relation to the content of which she is evidently not free. For in every point at which her visions present a clear contradiction to Rudolf Steiner's research, she decides not for anthroposophy, but for what is given her from out of her own body-bound sources.

In summary, one can say that in many places in J. v. Halle's books one can hardly suppress a feeling that is best expressed in the following words of Rudolf Steiner: 'One can think materialistically when one only grants relevance to the material aspect, and denies the spiritual – or also through pulling the spiritual down into the physical. One is likewise materialistic

when one only wants to accept the spiritual in material clothing'
(GA 130, 11 April 1911).

It goes without saying that J. v. Halle can communicate
the contents of her sense-bound visions to people wherever she
finds an audience. However, by ever and again making reference
to Rudolf Steiner in her lectures and books, and putting forward
her visions as being equivalent to his spiritual research, there
arises a problem to which one may not turn a blind eye.

*

Another particularly extreme case within this larger problematic
direction concerns visions of events at the Turning Point of Time
that are based solely on the sufferings of Jesus, as they are
depicted in the statements of A. K. Emmerich, T. Neumann and
in our time in J. v. Halle's books and lectures.[71]

What connects all three with one another is that – if
one here takes the words of Rudolf Steiner – they practice 'the
aversion of humanity's attention from the actual spiritual
dimension and its reorientation to the merely earthly-physical'
(GA 203, 27 March 1921) and want to guide their readers in
the same direction.

Rudolf Steiner dedicated a whole lecture to precisely this
problem, in which he explains how in the development of
Christianity from the fourth century on, the image of the
tortured and martyred 'Man of Sorrows of Nazareth' gradually
replaces that of the Risen Christ, which set the basis for Western
culture's later materialism: 'In an age when it is incumbent upon
man to experience the Resurrection of his own being in the spirit,
particular emphasis must be laid upon the Easter thought. We
must learn to understand the Easter thought in all its depths. But
this entails the realisation that the image of the Man of Sorrows

on the one side and that of the Judge of the World on the other, are both symptomatic of the march of Western civilisation into materialism' (ibid.).

Next, Rudolf Steiner presents in this lecture with great clarity how in earlier times – but just as relevant for our time – the one-sided devotion of human beings to the Man of Sorrows permeated by pain not only produced a turn to materialism, but acted in such a way as to block the true knowledge of the Christ Being: 'For the picture which from then onwards persisted through the centuries – the picture of Christ agonising on the Cross – is of the Christ Who could no longer be comprehended in His spiritual essence, but alone in His bodily-corporeal nature ... with the concentration on this picture of the Redeemer suffering and dying on the Cross, leave was taken of a truly spiritual conception of Christianity' (ibid.).

What has been said can also be expressed in an entirely different manner. One can also describe this tragic process in the midst of present-day humanity as the path back from Christ to Jesus. This tendency is in our time especially dangerous, because by its very nature – consciously or unconsciously – it is directed against the appearance of Christ in the etheric body, that is, in supersensible form. For the etheric Christ can only be perceived in a *spiritual* manner. And for this, a strengthened spiritual consciousness among humanity is needed. Rudolf Steiner said in this regard: 'We need, not the suffering Christ, but the Christ Who hovers above the Cross, looking down upon that which – no longer a living reality – comes to an end on the Cross.[72] We need the strong consciousness of the eternity of the spirit...' (ibid.). Precisely this consciousness is what Rudolf Steiner's anthroposophically-oriented spiritual science seeks to bring to modern people.[73]

It is also no coincidence that in this lecture he mentions the Eighth Ecumenical Council of Constantinople, of the year 869, in which the spirit was eliminated from the trichotomy of the human being. For when attention is directed primarily to the Man of Sorrows, there arises, to be sure, a mere duality: the image of the physically tortured person, and a soul-emotional relationship to it. Rudolf Steiner describes this as follows: 'Even in those days when human beings were not yet so dryly intellectual, so barren of real understanding, Good Friday still became a festival in which the Easter thought was transformed in an altogether egotistical direction. Wallowing in pain, steeping the soul voluptuously in pain, feeling ecstasy in pain – this, for centuries, was associated with the Good Friday thought' (ibid.).

Precisely this excessive and one-sided focus solely on the 'Man of Sorrows' from Nazareth, even going into cruel and terrible details (as is the case with A. K. Emmerich and J. v. Halle), leads unavoidably to the aforementioned voluptuous immersion in one's own feelings, which prevents the path to the Spirit of Christianity and thus to the Easter events; thereby, the Eighth Ecumenical Council begins to regain its entirely unholy power in humanity. What we need instead can be found in the above-cited words of Rudolf Steiner. We need 'the strong consciousness of the eternity of the spirit', through which alone one can come nearer to the Mystery of the Resurrection.[74]

Just how such a materialistic approach to the events of the Turning Point of Time concretely presents itself in our time, one may gather from the following. In an interview, the well-known film director Mel Gibson said that when he was preparing to produce a film about the last days of Christ on Earth, and read for this purpose the four Gospels, he initially felt he could not begin this project due to a lack of suitable material. However, once he became acquainted with books of A. K. Emmerich, there was no longer a problem for him. The result was that his film *The Passion of the Christ* (2004) evolved according to the 'Gospel' of A. K. Emmerich. It amassed world-wide more than half a billion dollars. This story is an additional testimony to what has here been characterized as the direction leading to materialism.

*

Also with respect to stigmatized people, the tendency described by Rudolf Steiner above is unmistakable. They are, due to the continual experience of their wounds, so strongly focused on the Good Friday events that an approach to the actual Mystery of the Resurrection remains as if closed to them.

One can observe this process especially clearly with A. K. Emmerich. In her major work, *Die bitteren Leiden unseres Herrn Jesus Christus* [*The Dolorous Passion of our Lord Jesus Christ*][75] she devotes more than two hundred pages to the events of Good Friday, seven pages to the events of Holy Saturday, but not even two pages to Christ's Resurrection.

One can likewise follow this tendency in J. v. Halle's written works. She reports very extensively and with terrible details about the events of Good Friday, and especially – similar to A. K. Emmerich – about Jesus' physical tortures. About the Resurrection she basically speaks very little. What is important about it, she borrows from Rudolf Steiner. And all that she herself adds to this is in parts quite problematic.[76]

That she actually has a big problem with the Resurrection is shown in one of her own statements. Here she tries to convince the reader (and in the process even sets the decisive word in italics) that with respect to the Resurrection body we actually have to do with something small, which in its effectiveness will last at most until the upcoming Jupiter stage, or even merely just ensure the transition to it.

Thus she writes (like probably everything else) from her own 'spiritual' experience: 'The Resurrection body is the physical form of the human being that can redeem and carry him from the seventh Earth-period of the mineral Earth-incarnation to the Jupiter-Earth.[77] The lowest element of Jupiter-Earth is the etherically spiritualized mineral Earth-kingdom. Only on Venus will the human being transform the members of his body to such an extent that he finally becomes Spirit-Man on Vulcan. That is the complete spiritualization of the body. In a certain sense, Atman corresponds to the physical condition of the human being during the Saturn stage. What could be described as physical body during Saturn, though in the most highly diluted, even "immaterial" state, a person will have transformed to Atman on Vulcan through the impact of his "I" and the work upon the lower members of his being' (*Von den Geheimnissen des Kreuzweges und des Gralsblutes*, p. 130 G [pp. 149-150 E]). And then follows the decisive passage, which due to its gravely serious content I permit myself to quote in italics: '*The Resurrection body, however, is* **not** [emphasis J. v. Halle] *the complete transformation of the physical body, as it will be developed in those distant stages, but is rather an illumination, a little pre-glimmer of this condition. It is the physical manifestation of the human being that conforms to the new, transformed Earth, which will emerge and spiritualize itself out of the mineral realm. It is a small process that takes place, corresponding to the great future events*' (ibid., p. 130 G [p. 150 E]).[78]

These words, which diminish the whole event on Golgotha and reduce it to something 'little', completely ignore the true cosmic dimension of Christ's Resurrection, which

85

includes the entirety of world evolution from ancient Saturn to the future Vulcan, and leads even far beyond that.[79] In addition, this claim of J. v. Halle contradicts quite clearly the results of Rudolf Steiner's research, which reveal a distinct connection between the Resurrection and the Vulcan stage of world evolution. It is neither 'a little pre-glimmer' nor 'a smaller process' as she says, but such an *immense process* that our whole imaginative capacity is actually powerless to grasp its true dimension.

I have never read, in any anthroposophical secondary literature, such a disparaging evaluation of the events of Easter Sunday.

Actually, these words by J. v. Halle speak so clearly for themselves that one hardly needs to compare them with the corresponding words of Rudolf Steiner in order to demonstrate their profound falsity. They show by themselves quite clearly that for her – despite all that she writes about it in her books – the true nature of the Resurrection body remains closed. It is for her '*not* the complete transformation of the physical body', and therefore no real Resurrection. The ground for this error has been given above. Her inner sight, her bodily experiences and the content of her visions relate primarily to the events of Good Friday.

However, for those readers who would like to see Rudolf Steiner's words at this point, I want at least to add a quotation concerning this matter here: 'We have here that Being, which embodied Itself in Jesus through the Mystery of Golgotha roughly halfway through human evolution – that Being Who was at the stage in world-evolution that humanity will have attained only at the end of Vulcan evolution. We have here the Being as God, which the human being will become at the end of Vulcan evolution as man' (GA 346, 7 September 1924).

From this statement it is clear that with respect to the Mystery of Golgotha, the main consequence of which is the Resurrection body, it is not a matter of the small transition from Earth to Jupiter, but rather of a process that spans the entire evolution from ancient Saturn (the place of origin of the Phantom) to the future Vulcan, and extends even until the 'end of the Vulcan evolution' (to the ultimate realization of the Resurrection body). Thus, at the end of this time the human being will indeed stand as fully developed Spirit-Man, insofar as he will have completed the entire seven-stage process of cosmic evolution. However, even at this stage as Spirit-Man, he cannot be equivalent to the Resurrection body of Christ at the Mystery of Golgotha, but will remain incomparably far below it.

Although at the end of the Vulcan period the human being will himself, through the long work of his human 'I', have fashioned the Spirit-Man element, this still remains a mere human creation. In contrast, the Resurrection body was created by Christ out of His divine 'I'. He worked in the process of its creation not as man, but 'as God', and that is something completely different, immeasurably greater and more comprehensive than all that the human being will ever create out of himself. For what is created by Christ extends far beyond Vulcan out into those spiritual worlds that for us today are still completely unimaginable.[80] With our brain-formed thinking we cannot even begin to grasp this tremendous dimension of the Resurrection, in the manner Rudolf Steiner describes it in relation to the seventh stage of Christian-mystical initiation.[81]

And yet, in our time the most important task lies in this: with the help of spiritual science, to come closer upon the path of cognition even to this central event of human and world evolution. In this sense, the claims of J. v. Halle – such as those cited above – lead in the opposite direction. Thus, they provide a clear indication that neither the stigmatization, nor the state of living without nourishment, amount to a guarantee for the veracity of the contents that a person disseminates publicly by means of the spoken and written word.

*

Among the many instances in J. v. Halle's books that either manifestly contradict Rudolf Steiner or appear altogether impossible for those possessing a Christian sensitivity, there must be added in closing a word about her attempt to reveal Rudolf Steiner's Mystery Name, which is, in addition, a false one. In her presentation, she points first to the strict Rosicrucian law, which states that the name in question may only be disclosed one hundred years after the death of the corresponding personality. Although this law – which Rudolf Steiner mentions in many places throughout his works – must still be respected for twelve more years in relation to Rudolf Steiner, J. v. Halle believes she can wilfully break it due to the conditions of the times, and that she is furthermore entitled to present the Mystery Name that she has contrived to the broad anthroposophical public already today.

Meanwhile, she provides only a few arguments to 'justify' her proceedings. She writes: 'One can observe namely that some occult laws, which have existed for a long time, indeed for centuries, have actually changed within recent decades. This is due to the tremendous acceleration of certain developmental processes, which are connected with the impending incarnation of Ahriman ... Thus, there seems to me in our time hardly any risk that one would speak too early about certain esoteric connections which come into consideration' (*Rudolf Steiner. Meister der Weißen Loge*, p. 91).[82]

The grounds that Rudolf Steiner gives for this law are, however, in no way to be relativized for our time – also and above all not in connection with the forthcoming incarnation of Ahriman, who will seek every possible means through which he can more effectively harm the great Christian Master as his main opponent on the Earth. For through the newest technical possibilities, and above all the Internet as the most pervasive world wide information-medium, much more harm can be inflicted on the initiate if his secret name is prematurely exposed than would have been possible in all previous centuries.

Before the words of Rudolf Steiner are presented here in which he describes this law – words which also allow the direction to be clearly perceived from whence his true Mystery Name will one day in the future be made known – one must bear in mind two aspects of his mission in connection to what he carried out with the creation of anthroposophy. In relation to the first aspect, he refers to anthroposophy as the 'Science of the Grail' at the end of his book *An Outline of Occult Science* (GA 13, Ch. VI), and then continues: 'The modern initiates may therefore also be called "Initiates of the Grail". The path into the supersensible worlds, the first stages of which have been described in this book, leads to the "Science of the Grail"' (ibid.).

When one further considers that in many lectures to members held during this time, Rudolf Steiner designated the seven stages of modern initiation – described in *An Outline of Occult Science* – as the Christian-Rosicrucian path,[83] then from this arises the second component to which his Mystery Name may have a connection.

To have these thoughts even more clearly present before us, the aforementioned context will be quoted here at some length: 'That which is contained in the Christian initiation was preserved in the symbol of the Holy Grail; it was brought into that community which imparts the Christian initiation. For those who receive the Christian initiation what is said here is not an abstract theory, not a hypothesis, but a fact of the supersensible worlds. The cultivation of the Christian initiation was entrusted to those who were the guardians of the Holy Grail, and later to the fosterers of the community of the Rose Cross.[84] What proceeds from the Christian initiation should, according to its entire nature, work in an impersonal way. Everything personal should be excluded from it; for the personal has brought only quarrels and strife into humanity, and will do this increasingly in the future. Therefore it is a strict rule for those who, symbolically speaking, serve the Holy Grail or, speaking literally, serve the cultivation of the Christian initiation, that none of those who have to play a leading part of the first order within the brotherhood of the Holy Grail or the community of the Rose Cross – neither they nor those who live in their surroundings – may speak of the secrets which they know and which work in them, before the passage of one hundred years after their deaths. There is no possibility of learning the complete truth about a leading personality of the first order until one hundred years have passed after his death. This has been a strict law within the Rosicrucian community since its foundation. Exoterically, no one knows who is a leader in the Rosicrucian community until one hundred years have passed after his death. Then what he has given has already passed over into humanity, has become the objective property of mankind. Thus everything personal is excluded. Never will it be possible to point to a personality in an earthly body as a carrier of the Christian Mystery. Only one hundred years after the death of such a personality would this be possible. This is a law that all brothers of the Rose Cross well observe' (GA 143, 17 April 1912).

Thus, every attempt to reveal Rudolf Steiner's Mystery Name prior to the passing of one hundred years after his death is highly problematic, because then the Rosicrucian law requiring strict adherence is broken; through this the bearer of this Name may encounter great difficulties in the spiritual world.[85] This indeed constitutes a very weighty betrayal of the spiritual foundation pillars of the Rosicrucian stream.

However, there arises yet another very serious problem when the name given is, in addition, false. For if one wishes to ensure quite definitely that a person will be separated from his connection to the spirit-individuality of Rudolf Steiner, there is a very good method of achieving this: namely, providing a false name, whereby people's thoughts will be led down a false path concerning this important question.

To still better understand what J. v. Halle is actually doing here, one must remember that Rudolf Steiner speaks about seven incarnated Masters of the White Lodge, but only names five of them. (See GA 264, 29 May 1915, pp. 204-205 G.) It was only at a later time that the leadership of the Theosophical Society – most notably C. W. Leadbeater – added two more names to the five already known, in order to complete the whole matter in an abstract scheme; there is, however, not a trace of this to be found in Rudolf Steiner's work.

This pertains to Leadbeater's book *The Masters and the Path*, having appeared in 1925, in which he brings each of the seven named Masters into connection with an inspiring ray from the realm of the Logos.[86] There the third ray is linked to the individuality known as the Venetian Master, and the fourth ray to the Master with the name *Serapis*. And precisely in this name, J. v. Halle wishes to see something that supposedly has a connection with Rudolf Steiner's esoteric name.[87]

To justify the Mystery Name that she found for Rudolf Steiner – that is, for the seventh Master of the White Lodge, which she believes him to be – J. v. Halle attempts to develop a strange etymology of this name from the Latin language.[88]

In order plainly to see the absurdity connected with this, one must turn briefly to the actual origin of this name. The name Serapis comes down to us from ancient Egyptian connections. It is composed of the names of two Egyptian deities: from Osiris, ruler of the world of the dead; and Apis, the name of the sacred bull of Memphis, the city in Egypt. From this there emerges the original designation: Osirapis.[89] The ancient Egyptians also sought the connection to their Time Spirit through the divinity who is concealed behind the figure of a bull, for the third post-Atlantean epoch stood under the guiding forces coming from the cosmic region of Taurus in the Zodiac.

After the founding of the city of Alexandria (331 BC) in northern Egypt by Alexander the Great, his successor Ptolemy I raised the Serapis-divinity to one of the principal deities. Behind this lay the attempt to maintain the strength of the high wisdom of the Egyptian time within the newly-emerging Greco-Latin epoch, and to integrate this high wisdom into the new epoch. Inasmuch as the primary language in Alexandria was Greek, the name Serapis is connected with the Greek language – and therefore, throughout several centuries, was also written with Greek characters (Σέραπις or Σάραπις).

At that time, however, the Mysteries of Osiris and Serapis – having still been so great in ancient Egypt – had already entered a state of full decline. This is indicated by Rudolf Steiner in the following words, by which he also confirms that the true Mysteries of Serapis belonged solely to the ancient Egyptian culture: 'Oh, these Egyptian Mysteries! Even by Alexander's time they were already so dampened down that they – I would like to say – were only like the slag from the wonderful old veins of precious metal, when there were still handed down from these Mysteries such profound teachings as expressed in the legend of Osiris, or in the worship of Serapis' (GA 237, 1 August 1924).

Later, the Serapis cult extended further north and west, and around the Turning Point of Time was among the most widely disseminated cults of the Roman Empire, which itself – as is known – had taken over much from the Greek-speaking culture. However, it is clear that at the time of the Roman Empire, the once so magnificent Ancient-Egyptian Mysteries fell even deeper into decline and became far more decadent than they were even during the Greek period.

It already becomes apparent from these facts that the attempt to find the etymological roots of the name Serapis in the Latin language completely overlooks the real origin, mainly because the Romans simply took this name from the Greek and from then on wrote it with Latin characters. And if one wishes to speak of a root-word for this name, then one cannot take this root-word from out of the Latin language, because 'Serapis' is not a Latin, nor indeed even a Greek word; rather, according to its origin it belongs to the previous Egyptian epoch and its language.

Nevertheless, in her book J. v. Halle undertakes an etymological 'analysis' that slips into fantasy. She brings the four letters 'sera', which she takes to be the root-word of the name Serapis, into connection with the Latin term for 'lintel' [a horizontal gateway beam; German: 'Torbalken'], which, like every lintel, rests on *two* posts – and then further, going beyond any etymology, relates this with the T-symbol in the sense of its meaning as TAO, apparently without noticing that a T has only *one* supporting pillar.[90]

93

Thus, her attempt to connect this name with Rudolf Steiner is completely arbitrary, and in a spiritual sense is absolutely false. For integrating the TAO wisdom into European culture was not Rudolf Steiner's mission, but rather one of the great tasks of Christian Rosenkreutz. Rudolf Steiner said in this regard: 'In 1459 it was Christian Rosenkreutz who recognized the necessity that the Tao-wisdom, in connection with Christianity, must bring about the new evolution. He brought the Tao or Rose Cross wisdom to the people of Central Europe, who had united themselves with the wisdom of the Old and New Testaments' (GA 264, 1 June 1907).

Rudolf Steiner's task, however, was connected with the triad IAO, about which he reported in an esoteric connection: 'IAO as the Name of Christ. This is connected with the Mystery of how Christ works within human beings' (GA 264, 'Individually Given Exercises No. 3236/37/38', p. 173 G). Precisely this was his task for our time: to reveal to humanity the Mystery of how Christ works in the human soul today. Furthermore, Rudolf Steiner connects this theme with Christ's words from the Book of Revelation: 'I am Alpha and Omega, the Beginning and the End' (Rev. 1:8), which is also connected with the triad IAO. For in one place he indicates Christ's Being as: *I* am *A* and *O*.[91]

From this may be understood a further task of Rudolf Steiner for our time: to proclaim to humanity the secret of the Resurrection body, which encompasses the complete evolution from ancient Saturn to Vulcan, from Alpha to Omega. He could do this only because he bore within himself in full consciousness the forces of the Resurrection body, and also acted and researched out of these forces.[92]

Appendices

1.
Comments Regarding the Book by P. Tradowsky

In 2009, a book directed against me by P. Tradowsky appeared in the Verlag am Goetheanum: *Stigmatisation. Ein Schicksal als Erkenntnisfrage* [English edition: *The Stigmata. Destiny as a Question of Knowledge.* Temple Lodge 2010]. At the very beginning of his 'Preface', the author indicates unmistakably to whom his remarks are directed: 'The present work is a kind of response to the Appendix of Sergei O. Prokofieff's book *The Mystery of the Resurrection in the Light of Anthroposophy* which bears the title "The Forces of the Phantom and Stigmatization"' (p. 7 G [p. 1 E]).

In what follows, I would like to go into just a few of P. Tradowsky's false assertions. The reader can refute most of them himself based on the above-mentioned Appendix in my book.

First of all, a remark about why the name J. v. Halle is not mentioned in this Appendix. (Upon the insistent demand of her supporters, this was compensated for in an Addendum to the English edition of *The Mystery of the Resurrection in the Light of Anthroposophy,* entitled 'Responses to Questions'.)[93]

My remarks were in no way concerned with the personal situation of J. v. Halle, her stigmatization or condition of living without nourishment, but rather only with the phenomenon of the so-called 'time-journeys' considered from an anthroposophical point of view. And because in this regard Rudolf Steiner only refers to A. K. Emmerich, her example was for me a given.

Regarding this my stance remains unaltered. With it, however, J. v. Halle was given the opportunity to distance herself from the somnambulistic experiences and visions of A. K. Emmerich.[94]

In my life I too am repeatedly exposed to criticism of my work, yet I have found that in reality the content of these criticisms has nothing to do with my statements. Therefore, it does not concern me personally. For an objective psychological law indeed applies here: He who is affected by a matter also has something to do with it. Thus, through her strong reactions to my comments regarding A. K. Emmerich, J. v. Halle identified herself with A. K. Emmerich's characteristic quality of being; moreover, her supporters carried out this identification for her by relating my criticism of A. K. Emmerich to J. v. Halle.

*

At the outset I would like to give an example wherein one can observe the grossly negligent manner in which P. Tradowsky works with baseless allegations towards me. He writes: 'The entire presentation of stigmatization by Prokofieff is based on a fundamental error, which is that he *implicitly and therefore unaccountably proceeds from the assumption* that the stigmatization is caused by the person concerned, and therefore could be removed again' (*Stigmatisation*, p. 13 G [p. 6 E], italics added).

In fact, I have related my statements, in accord with the descriptions of Rudolf Steiner, only to the fourth stage of the Christian-mystical path of initiation and in no way to permanent stigmatization. Hence, I never expressed such a thing as is claimed above, which P. Tradowsky himself even confirms: 'implicitly and therefore unaccountably'. The phenomenon of permanent stigmatization, on the other hand, has never really been of interest to me.

In our time, this whole difficulty has a particular explosiveness, inasmuch as at the heart of every contemporary relationship to the spiritual world, there must be ensured the full and inviolable freedom of each single person. This freedom is also to be found on the Christian-mystical path of schooling, because there, when correctly followed, the stigmata are evoked only voluntarily and temporarily through the pupil's exercises. (See the related quotations of Rudolf Steiner in Appendix 2 below.) Conversely, permanent stigmatization has nothing to do with freedom nor exercises, let alone a path of schooling, and thus also not with what in the sense of modern spiritual science will lead to legitimate research in the spiritual world – but rather leads only to such body-bound visions as are described by A. K. Emmerich and J. v. Halle.

Therefore, what P. Tradowsky describes as 'a fundamental error' (ibid.) on my part, is in reality a completely false allegation. For one can neither intentionally nor voluntarily eliminate a permanent stigmatization, and there I agree with him. This distinguishes it fundamentally from a stigmatization voluntarily evoked by corresponding exercises on the fourth stage of the Christian-mystical path of initiation, which only belongs to *this* stage and disappears of itself again after the exercises have been completed.

Inasmuch as J. v. Halle's biography is known well enough, one knows from it that she never in her life followed the Christian-mystical path in seclusion from the world, let alone practiced it up until the fourth stage, 'the Crucifixion'. She also surely did not tread this path even in the famous 'Canisius College' preparatory high school directed by Jesuits in Berlin, which she attended for two-and-a-half years.[95] From this one can conclude that her permanent stigmatization has nothing to do with the Christian-mystical path, upon which a temporary stigmatization is called forth voluntarily.

Hence, one can only agree with P. Tradowsky's following words: 'For those involved, stigmatization occurs suddenly and without warning as a pre-destined fact … [I]n principle, however, this concerns a life-event that as such occurs involuntarily, without the consciousness being involved' (ibid., p. 14 G [pp. 6-7 E]). Therefore, it is 'impossible to call it the result of some kind of asceticism, training or even research' (ibid.).

P. Tradowsky then summarizes his relevant observations as follows: 'All statements that connect the [permanent] stigmatization to following the Christian path of initiation are therefore irrelevant, and will not be dealt with further here' (ibid., p. 16 G [p. 8 E]). And that means precisely that these statements have nothing at all in common with J. v. Halle, with whose stigmatization his writing is concerned.

From this fact the very important conclusion can be deduced that a permanent stigmatization clearly has no connection with the Phantom of the Risen Christ. For all that Rudolf Steiner stated about the Phantom in relation to stigmatization concerns solely the fourth stage of the Christian-mystical path of initiation (see further details in Appendix 2 below), upon which stigmatization appears only temporarily – and to be sure, only during the time of the exercises.[96] Thus, seen from a spiritual-scientific point of view, J. v. Halle's permanent stigmatization, despite the many assertions of her supporters, is simply unrelated to the Phantom of Christ.

According to Rudolf Steiner, the Phantom that was restored by Christ in replicated form – and which since the Mystery of Golgotha passes over into all people who seek a conscious relation to Christ during their lives – by no means relates only to permanently stigmatized persons; rather, it concerns *all* people who have fulfilled the said condition in their earthly lives. (See also Appendix 2 below.)

In this respect, Rudolf Steiner says: 'So that *every Christian* must say to himself: "Because I am descended from Adam, I have a corruptible body as Adam had; but insofar as I bring myself into right relation to Christ, I receive from Him, the second Adam, an incorruptible body"' (GA 131, 10 October 1911, italics added). In another place he additionally expresses: 'To someone who contemplates evolution with occult sight, it is apparent that the spiritual cell – the body which overcame death, the body of Christ Jesus – has Risen from the grave, and over the course of time imparts itself to *every person* who enters into the corresponding relation to the Christ' (GA 131, 11 October 1911, italics added). In a third place he describes the 'spirit-body' of Christ as 'the body of which [the Apostle] Paul says that it *propagates itself like a grain of seed and passes over to all people*' (GA 131, 12 October 1911, italics added).

According to Rudolf Steiner's spiritual-scientific research, there are thus only two paths to the Phantom of Christ. First, the path for *all* people, who for this purpose must only find their relation to Christ; and second, the path through Christian initiation, which will only be taken by *a few*, and which Rudolf Steiner mentions in this connection in both of its forms: as the Christian-mystical and the Christian-Rosicrucian.[97] Permanent stigmatization and 'time-journeys' have nothing to do with this.

*

A second important consequence that emerges from what has been said – and which is likewise treated extensively in P. Tradowsky's book – is J. v. Halle's relation to two well-known permanently stigmatized people, A. K. Emmerich and T. Neumann. For with respect to many particular details, J. v. Halle's visions are the same as or similar to those of the other two stigmatics – a fact that W. Garvelmann has documented[98] in his book *Sie sehen Christus. Anna Katharina Emmerick, Therese Neumann, Judith von Halle. Erlebnisberichte von der Passion und Auferstehung Christi. Eine Konkordanz* [They see Christ. ... Experiential Reports of the Passion and Resurrection of Christ. A Concordance].[99]

In his book, P. Tradowsky compares the essential quality of J. v. Halle's experiences especially with the destiny of the permanently stigmatized T. Neumann, who lived in the twentieth century – and whose life is documented in much more detail than the life of A. K. Emmerich, who lived at the beginning of the nineteenth century. However, the comparison between T. Neumann and J. v. Halle, strangely enough, comes to a culmination with the curious words by which T. Neumann herself characterizes the condition she enters while receiving her visions. She explains, to be exact, 'Instead of her [Neumann] presenting information it is Christ (or her guardian angel or a saint) who speaks out of her. She in no way identifies herself with Christ, but she knows herself only as a medium through whom Christ works. As we know from the characteristic nature of her personality, because she possesses to an exceptional degree the ability to withdraw herself for the sake of the central idea of her life, it is quite possible for her, in a state of heightened rest, to totally obliterate herself in order to be nothing but just a medium' (*Stigmatisation*, p. 30 G [pp. 20-21 E]). Then he adds something of his own: 'As medium she is well aware of the duality between her person and her task' (ibid., p. 31 G [p. 21 E]).[100]

By citing these words, which P. Tradowsky also relates to J. v. Halle in his presentation, he demonstrates, as one of her closest supporters, what is actually involved with the phenomenon of permanent stigmatization and the resulting body-bound visions: namely, a special kind of mediumship[101] – which in any case has nothing to do with the present activity of the living Christ in His current etheric appearance, nor can it have any relation to this.

*

A further 'fundamental error' that P. Tradowsky believes he has found in my explanations is completely unfounded. For the problem I see in connection with J. v. Halle is not in her stigmatization nor in her state of living without nourishment, but solely and alone in the contents of her 'time-journeys', which she publishes in her books and which, as we have already seen, fundamentally contradict Rudolf Steiner and anthroposophical spiritual science in very many instances.

Inasmuch as J. v. Halle uses the results of Rudolf Steiner's research in order thereby also to augment them with her own – as she believes – spiritual-scientific insights, the situation regarding her publications and lectures becomes even more problematic. For it becomes ever more difficult to distinguish straightaway what comes from her body-bound visions, what she takes directly from Rudolf Steiner and what she gives as her own 'spiritual research'.

P. Tradowsky also refers to this characteristic of her writings: 'As of autumn 2004 Judith von Halle decided, after about six months, to speak about her experiences, whereby from the beginning her depictions were permeated with Rudolf Steiner's spiritual-scientific knowledge' (ibid., p. 9 G [p. 3 E]). And if one believes J. v. Halle that her body-bound visions began at

Easter 2004 with the appearance of the stigmata, then we have in the contents that she has divulged to the public since autumn 2004 – in the sense of P. Tradowsky's words quoted directly above – an impenetrable blending of her own presentations with the results of Rudolf Steiner's research.

The situation becomes even more dubious and confused when one here takes into account P. Tradowsky's following assertion: 'With the exception of the first publication [the book *Und wäre Er nicht auferstanden...*], the following publications have nothing to do with stigmatization; they result only from her capacity for spiritual-scientific work' (ibid., p. 11 G [p. 5 E]). Seeing that J. v. Halle's further publications are packed with her body-bound visions, and yet are held by P. Tradowsky and many others among her supporters to be 'spiritual-scientific work' – genuine spiritual research – then the confusion is now complete![102]

*

In what follows, I would like to address some specific allegations made by P. Tradowsky and at the same time refute them:

On page 22 [pp. 13-14 E], P. Tradowsky expresses that the true Cross on the Golgotha Hill had a Y-form. He claims that this is true because all three stigmatics (Emmerich, Neumann and v. Halle) have described it this way from out of their visions. Furthermore, he asserts that although Rudolf Steiner never mentioned the Y-form anywhere in his works, he also never confirmed the traditional form of the Cross. The latter, however, is not the case. For Rudolf Steiner says: 'Yes, indeed, it is possible to attain to the Imagination of the mountain on which the Cross was raised, that Cross on which there hung a God in a human body' (GA 131, 14 October 1911).

And it was precisely this Imagination that, at the beginning of 1915, Rudolf Steiner represented in the pastel sketch for the central motif of the painting in the small cupola of the first Goetheanum. (See the reproduction of the complete picture as frontispiece, as well as the corresponding detail from it on p. 47 of Chapter III above, where for the central Cross the † shape is clearly recognizable.)

Ten years later, at Easter 1924, Rudolf Steiner painted the watercolour 'Three Crosses. Easter', on which the central Cross likewise appears in the traditional form. With this he has given clear expression – not in words, but artistically – to how he saw the Cross on Golgotha in the sense of the words just quoted. The three Golgotha crosses are also depicted in the motifs of the violet and rose windows (here two times) in the north of the Goetheanum, in each of which the central Cross has an unmistakable † shape.[103] The †-form is also found in many of his blackboard drawings[104] – nowhere, however, a Y-form. Thus, one must conclude that all three stigmatics err in their visions with respect to this point.[105]

If one absolutely needs a written confirmation from the hand of Rudolf Steiner, then one can read the following passage from his book *Christianity as Mystical Fact and the Mysteries of Antiquity*: 'Plato relates it macrocosmically: God has stretched the World Soul upon the World Body in the *form of a Cross*. This World Soul is the Logos. If the Logos should become flesh, it must repeat the cosmic world-process in flesh-existence. It must be crucified and Resurrected.' Then Rudolf Steiner continues: 'The Cross on Golgotha is in fact the concentrated Mystery cultus of antiquity. This Cross comes to meet us first in the ancient world-views; we then encounter it within a unique event that is to apply for the whole of mankind, at the starting-point of Christianity.'[106]

Thus, for Rudolf Steiner it is in both cases a matter of the *same* figure of the Cross; that is to say, the figure in which two lines, directions or beams *cross* one another.[107] With a Y-form nothing crosses. For this reason alone, one cannot come to think of referring to it as a Cross-form.

*

On page 27, P. Tradowsky claims that in the administration of Rudolf Steiner's estate [Nachlass], the editors of Rudolf Steiner's complete works have not yet published his statements about the somnambulistic origin of A. K. Emmerich's visions 'probably because the editors were conscious of the uncertainty of the written record' (*Stigmatisation*, p. 27 G [p. 18 E]).

The actual fact of the matter, however, is that after 'Answers to Questions' were added directly to some volumes of the complete edition, this approach was later dispensed with and it was instead decided to gather all 'Answers to Questions' for publication together in a separate volume. As a basis for this, a comprehensive directory was compiled in which all the questions asked at the conclusion of various lectures, as well as the still-unpublished answers, were collected in one place. This directory can be viewed in the Literary Estate building by everyone. One can only hope that this content will appear in the not-too-distant future in a special volume within the framework of the complete works. Incidentally, the aforementioned statement by Rudolf Steiner concerning A. K. Emmerich was already published once before in a book by the Tombergian Robert Powell, which appeared in 1996 through the Anthroposophic Press in New York under the title *Chronicle of the Living Christ*.[108]

*

106

P. Tradowsky devotes an entire chapter to the issue of living without taking in nourishment. In fact, Rudolf Steiner said that the human being did not have need of physical nourishment before the Fall of mankind, and that the necessity for earthly nourishment came about as its consequence. (See GA 131, 12 October 1911). On the basis of these research-results, P. Tradowsky believes that the future path for humanity at the same time leads back to the original paradisal state, in which human beings once had no need of nourishment because the Phantom of the physical body was not yet filled with material and hence had no relation to earthly substance. For this reason, P. Tradowsky comes to the conclusion that not needing nourishment is a testimony (and even direct evidence) for the fact that the person in question carries within himself the Phantom of the Risen One.

However, the reality is completely different. The consequences of the Mystery of Golgotha do not lead humanity back to the original paradisal state, but to entirely new, higher levels of development, in which not the release from nourishment but rather the *spiritualization* of this process will play an essential role. Thus, the human being will take in physical substance in the form of liquid and solid nourishment until the Earth's full spiritualization at the end of Earth-evolution; however, he will learn to spiritualize this process from out of the force of what he will have acquired as image of the Christ-Phantom. Therefore, in this connection, a state of living without nourishment is out of the question.

Seeing that this represents the only appropriate developmental path, the Gospels tell us that the Risen Christ not only personally prepared food for His disciples and invited them to this meal (John 21:9 and 13), but even ate before them Himself.

The Gospel of Luke reports: 'As they still could not fathom it for sheer joy and amazement, He said, "Have you anything here to eat?" They gave Him a piece of broiled fish and a honeycomb, and He took this and ate before their eyes' (Luke 24:41-43). Naturally, the Risen Christ needed no nourishment for Himself. However, He ate in front of the disciples in order to indicate to them the direction in which earthly evolution must proceed in the Christian sense.

Had it been otherwise, such that living without nourishment actually was a Christian ideal, then the taking of bread and wine at the Last Supper would have been meaningless, that is, unchristian – which of course is not the case.

Likewise, Rudolf Steiner's great description of the cosmic communion, in the middle of which there are two meditations that portray the spiritualisation of the liquid and solid nourishment in human beings, would make no sense. For the cosmic communion, as he represents it in the lecture of 31 December 1922, leads precisely in the direction opposite the state of living without nourishment.[109] He connects this cosmic communion, which forms the heart of the cosmic cultus, with the central mission of anthroposophy, in that he says: 'That is the first beginning of what must come to pass if anthroposophy is to fulfil its mission in the world' (GA 219).

Even at the meal in Emmaus, the Risen One ate earthly food in front of those around Him. That, however, had nothing to do with the Phantom of the Risen One – which of course had to remain free of any physical substance – but with what Rudolf Steiner calls the 'etheric body condensed to physical visibility' of the Risen One (GA 130, 9 January 1912). Then he continues: 'We find it [the Emmaus scene] described in the Gospel not as an ordinary receiving of nourishment, but as a direct dissolution of the food by the etheric body, through the Christ forces, without the cooperation of the physical body' (ibid.).[110] This statement is especially important in this connection, because here Rudolf Steiner clarifies how such an intake of earthly substances occurred for the Risen One, and thus how it will come to pass in the future for all people who will work towards the spiritualization of the Earth.

*

P. Tradowsky devotes another chapter to the events surrounding Richard Pollak, who was also stigmatized. Although he actually followed the Christian-mystical path in his youth, the stigmata first appeared on him only in later years, and apparently had a permanent character. His wife, who had seen this on him, bore witness to it.

And then P. Tradowsky claims, without any foundation, that Rudolf Steiner's conversation with Richard Pollak, which I had conveyed and quoted, never occurred. The truth is, however, that Rudolf Steiner had already spoken with Richard Pollak about this earlier in Vienna, even before Pollak joined as an artist to take part in the building work of the first Goetheanum in Dornach. The anthroposophical painter Hilde Boos-Hamburger recalls her meeting with Richard Pollak as well as what Pollak himself related to her in this regard: 'Knowledge of higher life gleams from his eyes, in which great kindness shone. A deep seriousness and feeling of responsibility permeated his entire striving. It was years before the stigmata began to show and a great weakness tied him to his bed. At this time Hilde Kotanyi, his future wife, and I heard about Rudolf Steiner and asked him to visit. He came and said to Pollak: "This is no path for you!" and gave him indications that lead to the modern

Rosicrucian path. Years later Pollak related this to me. I often visited him and his wife in their studio in Vienna before 1914 and became friends with them.'[111]

*

At the end of this chapter, P. Tradowsky accuses me of emphasizing, in Pollak's tragic destiny (he met his death in Auschwitz), his moral qualities above all else. However, Rudolf Steiner also did this in reference to Francis of Assisi. In the many lectures he held about Francis of Assisi, Rudolf Steiner ever and again emphasized this moral greatness, yet not once did he mention his stigmatization. P. Tradowsky then declares that my esteem for Richard Pollak's purity and greatness of soul was the expression of 'a throwback to the realm of the "categorical imperative"' (*Stigmatisation*, p. 62 G [p. 47 E]) because I had supposedly established 'an ethical norm' (ibid.). However, that was not at all the case for me; rather, I simply expressed my greatest respect for the sacrifice of this so humble and deeply Christian person, who bore his difficult destiny with courage and devotion – still constantly helping other people – until his death in the gas chamber.

In this context it should also be considered that for the successful following of the Christian-mystical path, above all the astral body must be subjected to a thorough cleansing or catharsis, whereby – as in the case of Francis of Assisi – a high stage of morality is achieved. 'The re-fashioning of the astral body indirectly through meditation and concentration is called by an ancient name: "catharsis", or purification' (GA 103, 31 May 1908). In this respect, following the Christian-mystical path of initiation is connected with the highest degree of human moral development, which does not follow norms –

110

as P. Tradowsky seems to think – but reveals itself as a basic life-necessity, as is also shown in Richard Pollak's life.

*

Of course, P. Tradowsky is free not to regard Ita Wegman and Carl Unger as authorities in their assessment of the phenomenon of T. Neumann. However, when he quotes the following words of Rudolf Steiner from Ita Wegman's article about Kaspar Hauser: 'It was an attempt by the spiritual world to remind people, in the midst of a largely materialistic age, that there still exist entirely different matters other than what philistine thinking could dream of. And so there occur from time to time such wondrous events which one can understand only through a knowledge of the spiritual world; and these events, because they are so unfathomable, occupy all people and remind them again of the reality of the spirit' (*Stigmatisation*, p. 66 G [p. 50 E]) – and obviously brings this statement's relevance for our time into connection with J. v. Halle, then he should consider the following.

One can well understand that for 'the philistine thinking of people', who no longer believe 'in the reality of the spirit', such wonder-people might actually be needed in order to guide the attention again to worlds other than the physical. However, this should not apply for anthroposophists, who have learned so infinitely much about the spiritual world from Rudolf Steiner's research. If they did need such wonders and bearers of wonder in order to come towards the spiritual world, this would be a sign that anthroposophy had lost its entire meaning for these anthroposophists.

At this point, one should consider the following words of Christ to the people around Him about signs and wonders: 'But no other sign will be granted ... except the sign of the Prophet

111

Jonah' (Matthew 16:4). However, the sign of Jonah indicates an initiation. For he spent three days and nights inside a whale, which corresponds to the nature of the pre-Christian initiation. With regard to our time, these words of Christ mean that people should not admire all possible wonder phenomena. For what is valid in our time is solely the modern path of Christian initiation, as it exists in anthroposophy.

*

In his 'Afterword', P. Tradowsky further accuses me of falsely using the term 'Resurrection body' instead of 'Phantom'. However, Rudolf Steiner himself used the expression 'Resurrected body' in one place (GA 131, 11 October 1911), which means just exactly the same thing as 'Resurrection body'. In my book *The Mystery of the Resurrection in the Light of Anthroposophy*, the difference between the concepts 'Resurrection body' and 'Phantom' is covered extensively. The necessity of actually making this differentiation is confirmed by Rudolf Steiner's report that Christ had already completed the restoration of the Phantom on Good Friday. ('By the point at which this body of Jesus of Nazareth was nailed to the Cross, the Phantom was indeed fully intact, existing as spirit-body – though only in supersensibly visible form.'[112]) Therefore, Rudolf Steiner's spiritual research provides evidence that with Christ's Ascension on Easter morning, there happened a great deal more with regard to the Phantom than only its restoration.

And so one can speak of two states of the Phantom: the fully restored Phantom of Good Friday and the further transformed Phantom of Easter morning. This latter form of the Phantom I refer to in my book as the 'Resurrection body'. One could also say: the restored and the Resurrected Phantom

112

– or the Phantom of Good Friday and the Phantom of Easter morning. For here it is not a matter of a terminology question, but solely of comprehending what really happened with the Phantom during the Mystery of Golgotha. I think P. Tradowsky's confusion at this point is that he simply overlooked the above-cited words while occupied with the lecture cycle *From Jesus to Christ* (GA 131).

*

On page 70, P. Tradowsky also makes the following reproach: 'In this way Prokofieff tries to support his thesis that the stigmatization has nothing to do with the Resurrection, but only with the state of suffering preceding it, which is overcome with the Resurrection' (*Stigmatisation*, p. 70 G [p. 53 E]). That this is actually so, one can best adduce by considering the Christian-mystical path of initiation. There the stigmata appear – called forth by the spiritual pupil's exercises – only at the fourth stage, 'the Crucifixion'. We also learn from Rudolf Steiner's descriptions of the fourth stage that the appearance of the blood marks applies only to *this* stage, which is why he speaks of a 'trial by blood' (GA 97, 19 September 1906). However, nowhere does he indicate that the stigmata continue to persist at higher stages; for at these stages the pupil encounters quite other spiritual experiences, which in scope and significance far exceed all that has preceded them. This refers to the stages of the 'Mystical Death', 'Resurrection' and 'Ascension'. (See further about this in Appendix 2 below.) Here it should suffice to note that the Phantom as spirit-body following the Resurrection no longer bears wound marks; rather, these are only to be experienced on the condensed etheric body, because it is at the same time the memory body. (See note 110.)

113

*

On page 74, P. Tradowsky reproaches me with the following words: 'Prokofieff understands stigmatization as a reversion back to the situation of the Phantom before the Resurrection' (*Stigmatisation*, p. 74 G [p. 56 E]). But precisely this is the actual situation. For the wound marks on the physical body belong to Good Friday and not to Easter morning. After the Resurrection, the Phantom no longer bore any wound marks (what became of them has already been described elsewhere[113]). Everything that relates to the wound marks after the Resurrection belongs no longer to the Phantom, but to the condensed etheric body of the Risen One.

*

At the end of this section, I can say that with regard to this very last point I am in complete agreement with P. Tradowsky. And I was glad to see that in the final sentence of his book, he actually formulates exactly what for me is a matter of deep concern, what I truly think and want to represent in the world. Thus, I would like to close this first Appendix with P. Tradowsky's following words, for I will continue to stand fully and completely behind them: 'The message [of Prokofieff] is clear: Rudolf Steiner has the connection to the Resurrection body; the stigmatized Judith von Halle does not' (ibid., p. 75 G [p. 57 E]).

2.

An Incorrect Reference to Rudolf Steiner

In contrast to P. Tradowsky, who correctly makes a clear distinction between the permanent stigmata and the appearance of the wound marks on the fourth stage of the Christian-mystical path of initiation,[114] within some other publications by anthroposophical authors this difference is not recognized. However, it is essential to take account of this distinction in our time, because every step on the path of initiation is inalienably connected with human freedom. With the permanent stigmata, on the other hand, entirely different forces are active that clearly have nothing to do with human freedom.

Not long ago an essay was published in the Netherlands,[115] in which it is claimed that with the permanent stigmata (as they have appeared for Emmerich, Neumann and von Halle) one is indeed concerned with the fourth stage of the Christian-mystical path, and can even discover their origin in this stage. That is, however, not the case when this path is correctly followed – a fact which is substantiated in many descriptions of this stage in Rudolf Steiner's works. Some of them will be listed here.

As early as 1906, Rudolf Steiner spoke about the fourth stage of the Christian-mystical initiation: 'So can he [the spiritual pupil] call forth the stigmata on his skin during the course of his meditation' (GA 94, 1 June 1906). From this statement, it is apparent that only meditative exercises and an inner moral purification can cause the stigmata to appear on the pupil at this stage.

In another lecture from the same year, Rudolf Steiner comments in more detail about this: 'These exercises [on the fourth stage] lead to the vision that the pupil sees himself crucified, and this stage of initiation even reveals itself externally in that the so-called blood marks appear ... which can show themselves temporarily' (GA 94, 10 July 1906). From this quotation it is clear that the stigmata only appear on this fourth stage, and indeed temporarily – that is, as long as the pupil carries out the corresponding exercises. And just as the physical experiences of the previous three stages are not repeated in the higher ones, so the blood marks emerge only on this fourth stage. They are not carried forward to the three higher stages.

Rudolf Steiner speaks with even greater emphasis in yet another passage: 'This "trial by blood" indeed appears only for a few moments during meditation. Inner vision that one is oneself crucified' (GA 97, 19 September 1906). Here it is of additional significance that one does not see the crucified Christ, but experiences oneself as crucified. And in another lecture Rudolf Steiner says that the duration of the stigmatization on the fourth stage is only very limited: 'As external symptom, the blood marks – the stigmata – appear for a short time during the meditation' (GA 97, 22 February 1907).

That we here have to do with only one of the many trials that the neophyte must undergo on this path is indicated in another place: 'When a person has advanced far enough in this fundamental feeling [that his body is like a foreign object to him], what is known as the "trial by blood" shows itself on him. A certain reddening of the skin appears in particular places, in such a way that he can call forth the wounds of Christ'

(GA 99, 6 June 1907). Here it is emphasized that this is not a matter of bleeding, but only a reddening of the skin that the pupil voluntarily calls forth at five places on his body.

Also in another place, Rudolf Steiner speaks about such symptoms: 'During the time of meditation, stigmata-like red marks appear at precisely those places which are known as the sacred wounds' (GA 95, 3 September 1906). This is therefore not a matter of a form of blood loss, but rather an effect of meditation.

An especially important consideration regarding the appearance of the stigmata is found in another lecture, where one can read: 'Then there appears what is known as the "trial by blood". What in many cases can be a pathological condition is in this case a consequence of meditation, because all sickness must be eliminated' (GA 103, 30 May 1908-II). This statement is significant because it is here indicated that only when the stigmata appear as a result of conscious meditation can they be characterized as healthy; otherwise they could constitute a pathological condition, and that could be so 'in many cases'.

In a more general sense, Rudolf Steiner also reported that the Christian-mystical path is very old and has been followed by thousands of monks throughout the history of the West. 'There has been Christian initiation ever since the origins of Christianity and the time of the Apostles' (GA 94, 1 June 1906). In another lecture he adds: 'What I will say briefly to you now about this Christian initiation, hundreds and hundreds of people have gone through. It has become a practical experience for thousands' (GA 97, 22 February 1907).

One must call to awareness in oneself all quoted descriptions of Christian initiation – the number of which to be found in Rudolf Steiner's works could be still greatly increased – when one reads the last lecture of the cycle *From Jesus to Christ*, where

Rudolf Steiner points to his earlier detailed accounts before he once again characterizes the first four stages of the Christian path of initiation. Interestingly enough, he separates them from the last three. For these later stages demand a much greater effort and require a much more intensive training on the part of the neophyte than did the four previous stages.

He begins his presentation with the following words: 'What is attained by a man who thus seeks within himself to experience first the four stages, and then, when his karma is favourable, the others also – that is, all seven stages of Christian initiation?' (GA 131, 14 October 1911). Here the first four stages of this path (washing of the feet, scourging, crowning with thorns, and Crucifixion) refer predominantly to the person himself.

Yet already at the fifth stage – Mystical Death and Entombment – a person is able to leave his physical body in order to experience the spiritual connection with the whole Earth. Here, in addition to the human is added the much more comprehensive cosmic dimension of the event. This creates the path that leads from the human aspect of Good Friday through the occult event of Holy Saturday (the stage of the Descent into Hell), and gradually to the cosmic aspect of the Resurrection.

Therefore, Rudolf Steiner often mentions in his many descriptions of the Christian-mystical path of initiation that the seventh stage is not 'Ascension', but 'Resurrection'. Ever and again he speaks in this way about this stage: 'The seventh stage, that of the Resurrection, cannot be described in words. Hence in occultism one says: The seventh stage can be conceived of only by a person whose soul has been entirely freed from the brain. Only to such a person could one describe this. Therefore we cannot do more than mention it here' (GA 95, 3 September 1906). This is moreover that stage at which the ultimate union of the neophyte with Christ takes place. 'He is then wholly united with Christ Jesus; Christ Jesus is within him' (ibid.).

Not until this highest stage is a real union achieved with the Phantom of the Risen One, which received its definitive form not on Good Friday, but only on Easter Sunday. On the Christian-mystical path it is only at the final stage, the 'Resurrection', that union with the 'Resurrection body' really comes about. Therefore, Rudolf Steiner says in the last lecture of the cycle *From Jesus to Christ* that with respect to the lower stages, including the fourth, one can only speak of the very beginning, preparatory stage for the final union with the Phantom. He says literally that in this way we *'prepare ourselves* in our physical body gradually to receive the Phantom' (GA 131, 14 October 1911, italics added), 'that he [the neophyte] feels a *kinship*, a *force of attraction* to the Phantom' (ibid., italics added). These two statements follow directly after he has characterized the fourth stage of the Christian-mystical initiation with the appearance of the stigmata.

Then he describes briefly that in the Rosicrucian initiation, which is the only one appropriate for modern people, it is a matter of the same objective. There 'the same thing in a certain sense is also attained, only by somewhat different means: A bond of attraction is formed between the individual – in so far as he is incarnated in a physical body – and that which, as the actual archetype of the physical body, arose from the grave of Golgotha' (ibid.). Particularly this last sentence demonstrates that here it is a matter of union with the final form of the Phantom – a form which it had not yet achieved by Good Friday, but only on Easter Sunday when the Resurrection 'from the grave of Golgotha' occurred.

Following all preparatory stages on the Rosicrucian path, a real connection with the Resurrection body is possible only from the sixth stage onwards, in the Union with the Macrocosm – and that means in this context: in connection with the Resurrection body of Christ, which bears within itself all forces of the macrocosm.[116]

This arduous and difficult path to the *conscious* union with the Resurrection body, which is only possible on the highest stages of the two initiation paths mentioned, may not, as we have already seen, be confused with what is possible after the Mystery of Golgotha for every person without having undergone any spiritual schooling, simply due to an inner connection with Christ: namely, the generally accessible relation to the replicated images of the Phantom of the Risen One. (See above in Appendix 1, p. 101.)

From this, it follows that both of these approaches to the Resurrection body (through the aforementioned paths of initiation and through the relation generally accessible to all people) have nothing to do with stigmatization as such, and certainly nothing to do with the permanent stigmata.

For this reason, when more carefully considered, the attempt to link the permanent stigmatization with the activity of the Phantom of Christ, as is undertaken in the essay mentioned at the beginning of this Appendix, proves completely insubstantial. Moreover, the source of such thoughts is not spiritual-scientific knowledge, but rather certain wishes – which J. v. Halle's supporters project onto her and, as her own words demonstrate, which she herself encourages.

Inasmuch as Rudolf Steiner nowhere discusses the theme of permanent stigmatization throughout the entirety of his extensive works, and probably also consciously avoided it – as one can gather from the lectures dedicated to Francis of Assisi or his characterization of A. K. Emmerich, to which he was prompted only by a question – one can conclude that these states of being are unconnected with the acting of the Phantom, and can by no means be cited as evidence for such a relation.

3.
The Assessment of J. v. Halle by a Tombergian

In a rapturous, near-effusive manner, J. v. Halle and her writings are presented by leading Tombergian Robert A. Powell[117] before an English- and German-language readership. His book is called *Christ & the Maya Calendar: 2012 & the Coming of the Antichrist*.[118] J. v. Halle is spoken of at length in the final part of the second Appendix to the book, entitled 'The Good News'.

Before we briefly go into this, it must be mentioned that R. Powell had already become the topic of discussion many years ago when he named Rudolf Steiner a mere precursor to the *actual* Christian initiates. In one of his early books he made the following comparison between Rudolf Steiner and V. Tomberg – and to portray this even more blatantly, he based his comparison on the central figures of the Turning Point of Time.

He considered the former to be comparable to John the Baptist, as the forerunner of Christ; and by contrast, V. Tomberg with Jesus of Nazareth himself – that is, with that person who as a result of the Baptism in the Jordan became the bearer of the Christ Being on Earth.[119]

This comparison becomes even more impossible when one considers that John the Baptist, for all his greatness, was the last pre-Christian *initiate*. Jesus of Nazareth, on the other hand, was the first and only *Christ-bearer* in the entire history of mankind. Moreover, the whole matter is especially absurd because V. Tomberg left anthroposophy in the second half of his life and switched over to the Roman Catholic Church, and in his later publications publicly praised the Jesuit stream.[120]

Undeterred from this, R. Powell further develops this comparison directed against Rudolf Steiner in his book *The Most Holy Trinosophia and the New Revelation of the Divine Feminine*.[121] In it he writes that in the twentieth century three great teachers will appear: the initiate of the Father, that of the Son, and that of the Holy Spirit.

Although he does not at first mention the names of the three initiates, it is still easy to determine from his presentation that the initiate of the Father is supposed to have been Rudolf Steiner (accordingly, the representative of the pre-Christian Mysteries). The initiate of the Son and therefore the emissary of the Christian Mysteries is supposed to have been V. Tomberg. According to his opinion, the third initiate appearing in the near future, that of the Holy Spirit or Sophia, would have to be a woman.

That the whole presentation is in the most eminent sense directed against Rudolf Steiner and intended to contribute to his spiritual reduction – in order on this basis to highlight the alleged greatness of V. Tomberg who had converted to the Roman Catholic Church – is attested to by the following summary, which is developed in detail in the last chapters of R. Powell's book:

First Initiate (Rudolf Steiner)	*Second Initiate* (V. Tomberg)
Impulse of the Father	Impulse of the Son
Impulse of Michael	Impulse of Christ
Lesser Guardian of the Threshold	Greater Guardian of the Threshold
Old Testament	New Testament[122]

124

In his latest publication, which was mentioned above at the beginning of this Appendix, R. Powell goes even further. Here he also identifies the third initiate, who, however, should be female. He does so not in a direct way, but in a somewhat concealed manner. For here it is not a matter of this initiate himself, but of his 'messenger' or his 'public representative'. And this would be J. v. Halle.

R. Powell writes: 'Judith von Halle – although not identical with the third spiritual teacher in person – is nevertheless acting as a public representative of the third teacher who remains hidden behind the scenes' (*Christ & the Maya Calendar*, p. 236). And her task as such a 'representative' consists precisely in the fact that 'Judith von Halle's work is a fulfilment of that of the two teachers before her, bringing the work of the Etheric Christ a stage further at this crucial time in the twenty-first century' (ibid.).

These words sound so strange also because in most of her books J. v. Halle occupies herself primarily with the events of the Turning Point of Time, and only mentions the theme of the etheric Reappearance at most in passing. I do not know of a separate publication by her about this central anthroposophical theme. Thus, the thesis advanced by R. Powell remains without any factual basis.[123]

In this way J. v. Halle is brought by a Tombergian into the artificially conceived company of Rudolf Steiner *and* V. Tomberg (who later rejected anthroposophy). The whole situation becomes even stranger when one considers that the same R. Powell has published a 464-page book about the astrological background of the Turning Point of Time, based not on Rudolf Steiner but on A. K. Emmerich.[124] That is, still many years before J. v. Halle appeared, he published a book in which he presents readers with the results of Rudolf Steiner's strict spiritual-scientific research as well as A. K. Emmerich's body-bound visions – proposing them as equally reliable and mixing them together beyond recognition.

As we have already seen, almost all of J. v. Halle's publications suffer from just such a blending together of body-bound visions with the results of Rudolf Steiner's anthroposophical research. However, R. Powell has already gone down this problematic path long before her. And both aim basically in the same direction, the only difference being that R. Powell uses A. K. Emmerich's visions while J. v. Halle presents her own. However, the result is the same. Rudolf Steiner's anthroposophy is permeated by a fundamentally foreign, visionary element, whereby it can no longer be taken seriously in the world as a *science* of the spirit.

There can be no doubt that quite specific spiritual powers are at work behind this visionary element. This element can with certainty be excluded from anthroposophy. And it is likewise obvious that these powers are hostile to Rudolf Steiner and his entire work. For all subtle attacks on anthroposophy that lead to its distortion and even annulment are occultly intended, which makes the matters at issue in this book so grave.

Notes

1. See M. MOSMULLER: *Stigmata und Geist-Erkenntnis. Judith von Halle versus Rudolf Steiner* [Stigmata and Spirit-Cognition. Judith von Halle versus Rudolf Steiner]. Occident Verlag, Baarle-Nassau (NL) 2008; and F. BRAUN: *Die Stigmatisation Judith von Halles, deren – leider – falsche Aussagen und die Bitte an sie, nichts mehr bezüglich Stigmatisation zu veröffentlichen* [The Stigmatization of Judith von Halle, her – unfortunately – false statements, and the request to her not to publish anything further regarding stigmatization]. Niedenstein (DE) 2010.

2. Regarding this, see S. O. PROKOFIEFF: *The Mystery of the Resurrection in the Light of Anthroposophy.* Temple Lodge Publishing, Forest Row (UK) 2010. Appendix: 'The Forces of the Phantom and Stigmatization' and Addendum: 'Responses to Questions'.

3. M. WERNER / T. STÖCKLI: *Life through Light. Is it Possible to Live without Food? A Scientist Reports on His Experiences.* Clairview Books, Forest Row (UK) 2007.

4. Temple Lodge 2010 [Original German edition: Verlag am Goetheanum, Dornach 2009].

5. Temple Lodge 2010 [Original German edition: Verlag Freies Geistesleben, Stuttgart 2008]. The critical review by D. RAPP was published in *Das Goetheanum*, No. 6/2009.

6. For this see S. O. PROKOFIEFF: *Eternal Individuality. Toward a Karmic Biography of Novalis.* Temple Lodge 1992.

7. The problems associated with this are critically discussed by CORINNA GLEIDE in her essay 'Stigmatisation und Auferstehungsleib. Was heißt Auferstehung im Denken?' [Stigmatization and the Resurrection Body. What Is Resurrection in Thinking?], in *Das Goetheanum*, 'Nachrichtenblatt' [Members Newsletter], 7/2006.

8. Out of the same 'spirit', though not so directly, J. v. Halle relates a similar idea in her first book in the following words: 'Please believe me when I say to you, the Christ Being is speaking quite personally to you … I will always strive to bring to your heart the fact that His influence on me is a part of His loving impulse for *all* people!' In: J. v. HALLE: *Und wäre Er nicht auferstanden… Die Christus-Stationen auf dem Weg zum geistigen Menschen. Mit Beiträgen von Peter Tradowsky*. Verlag am Goetheanum, Dornach 2005, p. 37, italics J. v. Halle. [In English: *The Stations of Christ's Path to Spirit Man. With Contributions from Peter Tradowsky*. Temple Lodge 2007, p. 26].

9. Verlag am Goetheanum, Dornach 2008. Chapter: 'Das Geisteslicht am Ende des 20. Jahrhunderts' [The Spirit Light at the End of the Twentieth Century]. P. Tradowsky also writes about this in his book *Stigmatisation. Ein Schicksal als Erkenntnisfrage* (Dornach 2009) [In English: *The Stigmata. Destiny as a Question of Knowledge*. Temple Lodge 2010], saying that the stigmatized – including J. v. Halle – always 'cause violent pros and cons' (p. 17 G [p. 9 E]), and therefore bring with them a pronounced tendency towards division.

10. J. v. HALLE: *Das Mysterium des Lazarus und der drei Johannes. Johannes der Täufer. Johannes der Evangelist. Johannes Zebedäus* [The Mystery of Lazarus and the Three

Johns. John the Baptist. John the Evangelist. John Zebedee].
Verlag am Goetheanum, Dornach 2009.

11. Chapter 1: 'The Stages of Higher Knowledge' (GA 12).

12. However, J. v. Halle herself admits that her 'time-journeys' have nothing to do with Imaginations in the sense of the anthroposophical path of schooling: 'It is not therefore ... a matter of Imaginations' (*Das Mysterium des Lazarus und der drei Johannes* [The Mystery of Lazarus and the Three Johns]. Dornach 2009, p. 10). However, when in most of her books she mixes together her temporally displaced sensory perceptions with Imaginations taken from Rudolf Steiner's spiritual research, then something arises that truly harms anthroposophy.

13. This concerns the development of what Rudolf Steiner describes in various places throughout his works as pure or sense-free thinking, which must be achieved at this stage. For only this capacity is able to grasp the supersensible as such: 'That is the pure thinking, that kind of thinking which is not directed to external nature, but is solely directed to what is supersensible in man himself' (GA 293, 23 August 1919). And shortly thereafter he adds that here it is a matter of the 'pure sense-free thinking, in which the will is likewise always present' (ibid.).

14. For even just to reach the level of Inspiration, one must extinguish all previously experienced Imaginations in one's own consciousness through the free effort of one's will, so that one can thereafter live in a completely empty consciousness. In this way, the spiritual pupil removes himself further from everything that is somehow still connected with his physical body and sense impressions. This distance must be still immeasurably greater in order

129

to reach the stage of Intuition. For with Intuitive cognition an initiate can even research, in the spiritual world, the highest point between two incarnations of a human being. This is the so-called Cosmic Midnight Hour, when the soul – seen spiritually – is farthest from the Earth and its life in the physical body. The entire spiritual cosmos and the world of all nine Hierarchies lie in between and can be seen by the initiate only with his supersensible organs of perception. It follows that what Rudolf Steiner already said about the stage of Imagination (that it really has no connection anymore to any sense impressions), is intensified immeasurably with the transition to the stages of Inspiration and Intuition. From all this it is clearly apparent that the path of modern initiation and the path of 'time-journeys' proceed in precisely opposite directions.

15. Regarding the fact that the Phantom of the Risen Christ has nothing to do with stigmatization, see Appendix 2 below.

16. See GA 258, 16 and 17 June 1923.

17. Occident Verlag, Baarle-Nassau 2008.

18. For further details, see my book *Und die Erde wird zur Sonne. Zum Mysterium der Auferstehung* [And the Earth Will Become a Sun. On the Mystery of the Resurrection]. Verlag des Ita Wegman Instituts, Arlesheim 2012. Chapter 2: 'Das Sonnengeheimnis des Abendmahls' [The Sun Mystery of the Last Supper]. (English translation forthcoming.)

19. In a lecture in London about this topic, J. v. Halle even repeated the description of this scene in all its bloody details twice, which because of the gruesome nature of the depiction was for some listeners extremely upsetting and shocking. A young English woman reports about this: 'I went to Judith von Halle's lecture on The Last Supper

when she came to London. I cannot remember exactly when this was, but I think I was about 21 years old at that time.

Judith von Halle claimed to have witnessed the Last Supper in a clairvoyant vision, which formed the basis of her lecture. About halfway through the lecture she gave a graphic and chilling description of Christ sacrificing a lamb by slitting its throat, and smearing the blood of the lamb around the walls of the room. She then paused for a moment, as though gauging the reaction of her audience, before repeating the same description of Christ slaughtering a second lamb. I had the uncomfortable impression that she found these descriptions rather pleasurable, perhaps even thrilling.

My own reaction was one of hurt and anger that anyone could describe Christ in this way. The scene that she described seemed so fundamentally un-Christian that I had to conclude, if this were indeed an accurate description of the Last Supper, that Christ was not the God I believed in and I was not a Christian.

Some years later I read the Philosophy of Freedom for the first time, and in doing so I came to the view that morality is in fact Christ Himself. I remembered my reaction to Judith von Halle's lecture, and felt affirmed in my view that it is an impossibility for Christ to have behaved in the way she described.' (From a letter to the author dated 1 January 2013.)

20. M. MOSMULLER: *Stigmata und Geist-Erkenntnis. Judith von Halle versus Rudolf Steiner* [Stigmata and Spirit-Cognition. Judith von Halle versus Rudolf Steiner]. Occident Verlag, Baarle-Nassau 2008. Chapter: 'Zu: "Das Vaterunser" und

"Das Abendmahl'" [Regarding: 'The Lord's Prayer' and 'The Last Supper'], italics M. Mosmuller.

21. See S. O. PROKOFIEFF: *The Mystery of the Resurrection in the Light of Anthroposophy*. Temple Lodge 2010. Appendix: 'The Forces of the Phantom and Stigmatization'.

22. In the lowest realm of the Moon sphere, which borders immediately on the Earth, spiritual processes actually appear like physical-sensory objects, indeed so, as though one were perceiving them with bodily senses. This border area is however precisely the least suitable for true and error-free supersensible observations, because in the real spiritual world nothing more of a sensory nature exists. Hence, in the lower Moon sphere everything is like a kind of *Fata Morgana* [a form of mirage], which consists of an impenetrable mixture of illusion and half-truth, and is moreover usually influenced by quite problematic Moon spirits.

23. Even though in a slightly different way, the evangelists likewise drew their Imaginations from the Akashic Record. 'There is only *one* clairvoyant path to the Mystery of Golgotha, despite the fact that this event took place on the physical plane. We must keep that firmly in mind' (GA 139, 24 September 1912, italics added). In addition, all reports in the Gospels are connected with the Akashic Record: 'In the Gospels we have a reflection of the facts that are to be found in the Akashic Record' (GA 117, 14 November 1909).

24. See GA 95, 'Answers to Questions' regarding the lecture of 4 September 1906.

25. Regarding a fantastical description of the communion chalice, in which J. v. Halle largely follows A. K. Emmerich, see later in this chapter.

26. Many such passages are presented in the book by M. MOSMULLER (op. cit.) as well as in the book by F. BRAUN (op. cit.). See also S. O. PROKOFIEFF: *Und die Erde wird zur Sonne* [And the Earth Will Become a Sun]. Arlesheim 2012 (English translation forthcoming). Chapter 3: 'Das Gralsblut und seine esoterische Bedeutung' [The Grail-Blood and Its Esoteric Significance], and Chapter 4: 'Das Kreuz auf Golgatha und der Weltenbaum' [The Cross on Golgotha and the World-Tree] as well as the Addendum 'Responses to Questions' to the English edition of S. O. PROKOFIEFF: *The Mystery of the Resurrection in the Light of Anthroposophy.* Temple Lodge 2010.

27. J. V. HALLE: *Und wäre Er nicht auferstanden...* Verlag am Goetheanum, Dornach 2005 [In English: *And If He Had Not Been Raised...* Temple Lodge 2007].

28. See W. GARVELMANN: *Sie sehen Christus. Anna Katharina Emmerick, Therese Neumann, Judith von Halle. Erlebnisberichte von der Passion und der Auferstehung Christi. Eine Konkordanz* [They see Christ. Anna Katharina Emmerich, Therese Neumann, Judith von Halle. Experiential Reports of the Passion and Resurrection of Christ. A Concordance]. Verlag am Goetheanum, Dornach 2008.

29. The first stigmatized person in the history of Christianity, however, Francis of Assisi (1182–1226), received his stigmatization from an image of Christ, in which Christ in the form of a Seraph was crucified on a right-angled Cross. See also the picture by Giotto, 'The Stigmatization of St. Francis' in the Capella Bardi, Chiesa di Santa Croce, Florence.

30. See in Chapter 4: 'Das Kreuz auf Golgatha und der Weltenbaum' [The Cross on Golgotha and the World-Tree]. Arlesheim 2012.

31. J. V. Halle: essay 'Die Erlösergeste Christi' [The Redeeming Gesture of Christ]. *Das Goetheanum*, No. 15/16, 2009.

32. See also Mark 15:33 and Luke 23:44. All quotations from The New Testament are based on *The New Testament. A Rendering by Jon Madsen*. Floris Books (UK), 2006.

33. J. V. Halle: essay 'Das Zeugnis des Lichts' [The Testimony of Light]. *Das Goetheanum*, No. 1/2, 2008.

34. A. K. Emmerich: *Das erste Lehrjahr Jesu* [The First Year of Jesus as Teacher]. Stein am Rhein, 2004. Chapter 3, p. 137.

35. See P. Selg: *Das Ereignis der Jordantaufe. Epiphanias im Urchristentum und in der Anthroposophie Rudolf Steiners* [The Event of the Jordan Baptism. Epiphany in Early Christianity and the Anthroposophy of Rudolf Steiner]. Verlag Freies Geistesleben, Stuttgart 2008, as well as the depiction of the Baptism scene in the Goetheanum's southern blue window and the corresponding sketch for it by Rudolf Steiner.

36. In two other lectures, Rudolf Steiner also points out that above all the motifs of the Madonna with Child and 'Christ on the Cross' had their source here. (See GA 109, 7 March 1909 and 6 April 1909.) This is further proof that the Cross on Golgotha had the †-form.

37. Essay titled 'Gnosis and Anthroposophy'. It is not without significance that this description of the Grail is not derived from a lecture – where the possibility of a mistake occurring in the transcription or in notes written from memory cannot be ruled out – but from a handwritten presentation by Rudolf Steiner.

38. See J. V. Halle: *Das Abendmahl. Vom vorchristlichen Kultus zur Transsubstantiation* [The Last Supper. From Pre-Christian Cultus to Transubstantiation]. Verlag am

Goetheanum, Dornach 2006. Chapter: 'Der Kelch – seine belebte Substanz und Gestalt' [The Chalice – Its Living Substance and Form].

39. See A. K. EMMERICH: *Das bittere Leiden unseres Herrn Jesus Christus.* Stein am Rhein, 2006. Chapter: 'Vom Kelch des heiligen Abendmahles', p. 62. [In English: *The Dolorous Passion of Our Lord Jesus Christ.* TAN Books and Publishers, Rockford Illinois (USA), 1994. Meditation IV: 'The Chalice Used at the Last Supper'.]

40. The contradiction is that the fifth layer of the Earth consists of 'living matter', which belongs to the original condition of the Earth-era and not to the previous era of Old Moon.

41. J. V. HALLE: *Der Abstieg in die Erdenschichten.* Verlag am Goetheanum, Dornach 2008, p. 74. [In English: *Descent into the Layers of the Earth.* Temple Lodge 2011, pp. 66-67.]

42. Literally, Rudolf Steiner says: 'In this [sixth] layer there works, substantively and in essence, the realm of Ahriman; from this layer he is active. ... That is the centre of his activity' (GA 107, 1 January 1909).

43. J. V. HALLE: *Und wäre Er nicht auferstanden...* Verlag am Goetheanum, Dornach 2005 [In English: *And If He Had Not Been Raised...* Temple Lodge 2007]. Cf. the description of A. K. Emmerich in her book *Das bittere Leiden unseres Herrn Jesus Christus.* Stein am Rhein, 2006. Chapter: 'Jesus am Ölberg', pp. 90-92. [In English: *The Dolorous Passion of Our Lord Jesus Christ.* TAN Books 1994. Chapter 1: 'Jesus in the Garden of Olives'.]

44. J. V. HALLE: Ibid.

45. J. V. HALLE: Ibid. In the descriptions of A. K. Emmerich, this process is described as follows: 'And the angels gathered in a mysterious way all the sacred substances which were taken

from Him [the Lord] in His sorrow ... I observed how the body of the Lord rested again in the holy grave and, as with everything that had been snatched from Him during the torture, was completed in a mysterious way by the angels' (*Das bittere Leiden unseres Herrn Jesus Christus*. Stein am Rhein, 2006. Chapter: 'Nacht vor der Auferstehung'). [In English: *The Dolorous Passion of Our Lord Jesus Christ*. TAN Books 1994. Chapter 60: 'The Eve of the Resurrection'.]

46. See also in S. O. PROKOFIEFF: *Und die Erde wird zur Sonne* [And the Earth Will Become a Sun]. Arlesheim 2012. Chapter 3: 'Das Gralsblut und seine esoterische Bedeutung' [The Grail-Blood and Its Esoteric Significance]. About the path of the Phantom after death, see S. O. PROKOFIEFF: *The Mystery of the Resurrection in the Light of Anthroposophy*. Temple Lodge 2010. Chapter: 'The Mystery of Golgotha and Spiritual Communion', as well as in *Und die Erde wird zur Sonne*, Chapter 5: 'Das Erscheinen der Toten im Matthäus-Evangelium' [The Appearance of the Dead in the Gospel of Matthew].

47. See especially Rudolf Steiner's lectures about *The Fifth Gospel* (GA 148) as well as the lecture of 9 January 1912, in GA 130.

48. Rudolf Steiner reports about this: 'Since the moment when the cosmic Christ-Being had been present at the Baptism by John, it is evident that no forces of attraction arose between the human Phantom and what was taken up as material part [in it]. Throughout all three years, the Phantom remained unaffected by the material elements' (GA 131, 12 October 1911).

49. See Note 46.

50. In the lecture cycle *From Jesus to Christ*, Rudolf Steiner uses

Rosicrucian-alchemical terms to describe this process of volatilization of the bodily substances. According to his description, the Phantom develops a strong force of attraction in relation to the dissolving salt-components of the body, but not in relation to its solid ash-components. (See GA 131, 12 October 1911.)

51. See the above-mentioned essay by J. V. HALLE: 'Die Erlösergeste Christi' [The Redeeming Gesture of Christ].

52. See W. GARVELMANN: *Sie sehen Christus. Anna Katharina Emmerick, Therese Neumann, Judith von Halle... Eine Konkordanz* [They See Christ. ... A Concordance]. Dornach 2008. Again, it is striking here that J. v. Halle follows not Rudolf Steiner and his spiritual research, but solely her own visions.

53. J. V. HALLE: *Und wäre Er nicht auferstanden...* Verlag am Goetheanum, Dornach 2005 [In English: *And If He Had Not Been Raised...* Temple Lodge 2007]. Since J. v. Halle additionally refers in this context (p. 153 G [p. 132 E]) to the famous painting by Matthias Grünewald (*The Resurrection of Christ* from the Isenheim Altar), it must be mentioned that she is also wrong here. With a closer consideration of the painting, one can see that the movement does not pass through the stone, but occurs *in front* of it with the stone in the background.

54. In another lecture Rudolf Steiner also reported a 'mighty whirlwind', which caused the unusual arrangement of the shrouds in the grave. (See GA 148, 18 December 1913.)

55. The fact that the restored Phantom was free from all earthly material and also no longer limited by time and space – being a purely spiritual form – belonged to its nature from the beginning. The Gospels also provide decisive indication

of this: for example, in the passage in the Gospel of John where it is said: 'On the evening of that day, the first day of the Sabbath, the disciples *had locked the doors of the room* where they were, for fear of the Jews. Then Jesus came and stood in their midst...' (John 20:19, italics added). That Christ could go through a locked door in this case has nothing to do with any kind of magic, but solely with the nature of the Phantom itself. In contrast, the stories about material cloths that move through the matter of a stone do not belong in this context.

56. It is precisely for this reason that Rudolf Steiner presented – in the cycle *From Jesus to Christ* – the comparison between Christ Jesus and His contemporary, the famous adept, magician, and miracle-worker Apollonius of Tyana (he died at an advanced age in the year 120 A.D.), of whom tradition says that he accomplished countless miracles with his magic arts. (See GA 131, 7 October 1911.)

57. In the Gospels, it was in Christ Jesus' close circle only Judas Iscariot who hoped for such a magical working by the Christ, in order to see his twisted messianic delusions fulfilled. Also the Jewish priests and scribes, who mocked the Crucified One on the Hill of Golgotha, said: 'He helped others, but He cannot help Himself. He is the King of Israel; very well, let Him come down from the Cross and we will believe in Him' (Matthew 27:42). They meant this as a provocation, so that Christ Jesus might show Himself not as the true Messiah, but as a great magician.

58. In this regard see the example from J. v. Halle's lecture and book, which I have discussed above at the end of Chapter II.

59. See in further detail in S. O. PROKOFIEFF: *Und die Erde wird zur Sonne* [And the Earth Will Become a Sun]. Arlesheim

2012. Chapter 6: 'Das Weltenschicksal des Bösen' [The World-Destiny of Evil].

60. J. V. HALLE: *Das Mysterium des Lazarus und der drei Johannes* [The Mystery of Lazarus and the Three Johns]. Dornach 2009.

61. Rudolf Steiner reports in this regard: 'John, the brother of James and son of Zebedee, is not an Apostle in the actual sense' (GA 264, Section: 'Aus dem Lehrgut über die Meister der Weisheit und des Zusammenklanges der Empfindungen' [From the Teachings about the Masters of Wisdom and of the Harmony of Feelings], p. 232 G). And then he makes an even clearer statement about this in a private conversation: 'Did Zebedee's sons belong at all to the circle of twelve? In the Zodiac, in which Christ saw His nature reflected? This must be a mistake if it is to be found in the Gospels' (GA 264, ibid., p. 239 G).

62. For example, in fatal traffic accidents.

63. Moreover, precisely in the case of the great initiates, one has to do with the opposite tendency. In such cases the body remains uncorrupted after death, even for centuries. Perhaps the most important example of this nature (alongside various saints and yogis) is the discovery of the completely intact body of Christian Rosenkreutz one hundred years after his death, as is described by Johann Valentin Andreae in the *Fama Fraternitatis* (reprinted in P. SELG: *Rudolf Steiner and Christian Rosenkreutz*. SteinerBooks 2012, Ch. 3).

64. The 'I' of John, son of Zebedee – who according to J. v. Halle had suddenly disappeared from the physical plane – united itself, according to her, with the body of his brother James, who thereafter represented them both within the

circle of disciples as a composite-essence of the two. For this reason the author speaks of 'James-John-Zebedee' as one single person, perceptible to the senses: 'It is just this "James-John-Zebedee" who received access and entrance into the closest circle of Twelve, into the Zodiacal Circle' (*Das Mysterium des Lazarus...*, p. 133).

65. J. V. HALLE: *Das Mysterium des Lazarus und der drei Johannes* [The Mystery of Lazarus and the Three Johns]. Dornach 2009.

66. Rudolf Steiner speaks about such an initiation being a matter of a 'three-and-a-half-day deathlike sleep' in GA 103, 22 May 1908.

67. In the book mentioned, Rudolf Steiner dedicates a whole chapter to this theme: 'The Lazarus Miracle' (GA 8). This book was published as a summary of the lectures that Rudolf Steiner held in Berlin in winter 1901/1902. Furthermore, he dedicates an entire lecture to Lazarus' initiation in the cycle about the Gospel of John (GA 103, 22 May 1908). The last time Rudolf Steiner mentions the *initiation* of Lazarus is in his 'Last Address', in which he narrates John's spiritual experiences 'as he is transformed from Lazarus into John *through the initiation of Christ Jesus*' (GA 238, 28 September 1924, italics added). Thus, this theme runs like a common thread throughout all his work, which shows its special importance, also for Rudolf Steiner himself.

68. Regarding this, see S. O. PROKOFIEFF: *May Human Beings Hear It! The Mystery of the Christmas Conference*. Temple Lodge 2004. Chapter 9: 'The Foundation Stone Meditation. Karma and Resurrection', as well as S. O. PROKOFIEFF: *Die Esoterik der Anthroposophischen Gesellschaft* [The

Esotericism of the Anthroposophical Society]. Verlag am Goetheanum, Dornach 2012. (English translation forthcoming. In this regard, see also Chapter 8 of *May Human Beings Hear It!*)

69. Rudolf Steiner's spoken explanation of his 'Last Address'. See GA 238, 'Ergänzende Bemerkungen' [Additional Remarks] in the 1981 [German] edition.

70. In addition to the two books already mentioned in Note 1, see the following essay: C. GLEIDE: 'Was heißt Auferstehung im Denken?' [What Is Resurrection in Thinking?], *Das Goetheanum*, 'Nachrichtenblatt' [Members Newsletter], 7/2006, as well as the essay by M. MOSMULLER: 'Die Frage nach Wundern und solchen, die nicht sein können...' [The Question of Wonders and Such Things that Could Not Be...] in the magazine *Der Europäer*, No. 2/3, December/January 2009/2010, and the essay by RICHARD RAMSBOTHAM: 'Chinese Whispers'. In: *Der Europäer*, No. 4, February 2011.

71. Cf. W. GARVELMANN: *Sie sehen Christus. Anna Katharina Emmerick, Therese Neumann, Judith von Halle... Eine Konkordanz* [They See Christ. ... A Concordance]. Dornach 2008.

72. Rudolf Steiner represented artistically just this relation of Christ to Jesus in his pastel sketch for the central motif of the painting in the small cupola of the first Goetheanum (see frontispiece).

73. One can find the basis for an experience and cognitive understanding of Easter particularly within Rudolf Steiner's Christological work, where he presents Christ as a super-earthly, cosmic Being. In the lectures on the Fifth Gospel (GA 148), Rudolf Steiner brings the cosmic into connection

with the earthly in an especially impressive way, but such that the cosmic aspect is not thereby lost. About this, see also S. O. PROKOFIEFF: *Und die Erde wird zur Sonne* [And the Earth Will Become a Sun]. Arlesheim 2012. Chapter 7: 'Das Fünfte Evangelium und die gegenwärtige Christus-Erkenntnis' [The Fifth Gospel and the Christ-Cognition of the Present Time].

74. Here I would like sincerely to encourage the reader to read this lecture by Rudolf Steiner, of 27 March 1921 (GA 203), once in its entirety.

75. Stein am Rhein, 2006; Volume 5 of the complete edition [In English: TAN Books 1994].

76. See an example on p. 152 G [p. 130-132 E] of *Und wäre Er nicht auferstanden...*, where J. v. Halle describes how a material cloth passes through the substance of a stone. (See p. 63 of Chapter III above).

77. On the opposite page in her book *Von den Geheimnissen des Kreuzweges...*, p. 131 G [151 E], J. v. Halle prints a diagram that is supposed to illustrate this difficult sentence. There she draws seven large 'time-periods of the Earth', two of which (the sixth and seventh) still lie in the future, preceding the end of Earth-evolution. Then the Earth will be dissolved. After the seventh period, the Earth is transformed into Jupiter. This transition from the seventh (last) Earth-condition to Jupiter is indicated on the diagram by an arrow, above which the words 'Resurrection body' are written. This shows vividly once more that J. v. Halle sees the effectiveness of the Resurrection body only up until Jupiter. The whole matter is further reinforced by the text under the diagram, which reads: 'The Resurrection body as *first step* towards spiritualizing the body' (italics added).

78. Quoted from J. v. HALLE: *Von den Geheimnissen des Kreuzweges und des Gralsblutes.* Dornach 2006 [In English: *Secrets of the Stations of the Cross and the Grail Blood.* Temple Lodge 2007].

79. See GA 346, 7 September 1924 and S. O. PROKOFIEFF: *The Mystery of the Resurrection in the Light of Anthroposophy.* Temple Lodge 2010. Chapter 2: 'Easter, Ascension and Whitsun in the Light of Anthroposophy'.

80. See further in S. O. PROKOFIEFF: Ibid., Ch. 2.

81. See his statement quoted on p. 118 in Appendix 2 below (quotation from GA 95: 3 September 1906).

82. J. v. HALLE: *Rudolf Steiner. Meister der Weißen Loge. Zur okkulten Biographie* [Rudolf Steiner. Master of the White Lodge. An Occult Biography]. Verlag für Anthroposophie, Dornach 2011.

83. See e.g. GA 97: 19 September 1906, 30 November 1906 and 11 December 1906; and GA 99: 6 June 1907.

84. In this passage as well as in some others in his work, Rudolf Steiner speaks quite clearly about the fact that the Mysteries of the Grail were adopted in later times by the Rosicrucians and flowed from there into anthroposophy. The Grail Mysteries have nothing to do with other Western esoteric streams, as for example the Templars.

85. Rudolf Steiner speaks about such difficulties in the lectures of 27 September 1911, and 27 January 1912 (GA 130), as well as in the lecture of 24 April 1912 (GA 133).

86. Quest Books, Adyar 1985. To be sure, all seven names were already known within the Theosophical Society; however, Leadbeater was the first to summarize their activities and relationships to one another in a clear way. Somewhat later, Alice Bailey took up his theory and developed it further in

her book *Initiation. Human and Solar*. Lucis Press, New York/London 1984. Regarding this, see also S. O. Prokofieff: *The East in the Light of the West. Parts One to Three*. Temple Lodge 2009. Part 2: 'The Teachings of Alice Bailey in the Light of Christian Esotericism'.

87. See J. v. Halle: *Rudolf Steiner. Meister der Weißen Loge* [Rudolf Steiner. Master of the White Lodge]. Dornach 2011, pp. 134-135.

88. In her book this name is introduced in the following way: 'For this reason, for a long time one has used an especially abstract-sounding "place holder" for the individuality of the seventh Master; that is the name *Serapis*' (pp. 134-135, italics J. v. Halle). She speaks in this connection about the 'place-holder name Serapis' (ibid.). Her contention that Rudolf Steiner *is* the seventh Master of the White Lodge was based on notes by Edith Maryon, which are provided at the end of her book. In these notes, however, a clear distinction is made between Rudolf Steiner as spiritual teacher, and the Master of the White Lodge who speaks through him. Edith Maryon writes: 'This means drawing a clear line between a statement and a statement of the Master of the White Lodge. It is, however, the Doctor's task that within him the seventh Master may unfold his working' (ibid., pp. 160-161). In a similar manner Elisabeth Vreede mentions in her lectures 'Zur Boddhisattva-Frage' [On the Bodhisattva Question] that she experienced during an Esoteric Class Lesson in 1909 how Zarathustra (Master Jesus) spoke out of and through Rudolf Steiner. Thereby, she could feel – through the working of Rudolf Steiner – that the spiritual individuality of this Master was directly in the same room. This happened in just the same way in other situations – according to

Edith Maryon – likely also with the seventh Master.

89. This Egyptian-Greek etymology can be found, among others places, in the following book by Clement of Alexandria, who lived in the second century and who before his acquaintance with Christianity was initiated into many ancient Mysteries: *Ein Wort an die Heiden* [A Word to the Pagans]. (See the Russian translation, Chapter XLVIII, 'Die Geschichte des Serapis-Standbildes' [The History of the Serapis Statue], St. Petersburg 2010.) Rudolf Steiner speaks with great respect about Clement of Alexandria in many places throughout his work. It is reported of Clement that he could read Egyptian hieroglyphs and had mastered the Egyptian language of the time.

90. See J. v. HALLE: *Rudolf Steiner. Meister der Weißen Loge* [Rudolf Steiner. Master of the White Lodge]. Dornach 2011, p. 135.

91. See GA 127, 26 December 1911.

92. See further details about this in Appendix 2 below. What has been said does not, however, exclude the possibility that Edith Maryon was correct, and that the seventh Master in fact also worked through Rudolf Steiner. This truth, in the event that Edith Maryon was correct, still has nothing to do with J. v. Halle's claim that Rudolf Steiner's esoteric name is 'Serapis'. About this Edith Maryon did not write one word.

93. In German, this Addendum first appeared in the book *Und die Erde wird zur Sonne* [And the Earth Will Become a Sun]. This book was published in 2012 through the Verlag des Ita Wegman Instituts in Arlesheim, Switzerland, after it was already long-announced by the Verlag Freies Geistesleben in Stuttgart, Germany. The publication was, however, finally rejected by Verlag Freies Geistesleben.

94. See further in the aforementioned Addendum regarding the authenticity of Rudolf Steiner's statement about the somnambulistic sources of A. K. Emmerich's visions.

95. For this, see the yearbooks titled *Unsere Schule* [Our School] of Canisius College, Berlin, volumes 1988 and 1989, with the offers presented there for various intellectual and extracurricular activities. In both books, J. v. Halle is mentioned as student by her maiden name.

96. In the lecture of 14 October 1911 (GA 131), Rudolf Steiner also mentions that the second path towards achieving a connection with the Resurrection body in our time is the Christian-Rosicrucian initiation. In this connection, one must really make conscious for oneself what J. v. Halle states about her own 'so-called' path of schooling: 'After the publication of my lectures in book-form, several people have requested a clear description of my so-called path of schooling' (J. v. HALLE: *Das Mysterium des Lazarus...*, op. cit. p. 13). She then notes that 'such a "construction manual" [would be] very short and probably not the way these people imagine or would want' (ibid., p. 13).

97. If one reads this precise point in the cycle *From Jesus to Christ*, one will notice that in describing the relation of all people to the Phantom, Rudolf Steiner says at the same time that it 'propagates' itself like a grain of seed. Here it is a matter of the person receiving only an image of the replicating Phantom into himself (see GA 131, 12 October 1911). In the last lecture within this cycle, where Rudolf Steiner speaks about the relation of the two paths of initiation to the Phantom, he does not mention the word 'propagation', but ever and again speaks about the direct relation of the neophyte to the Resurrection body of Christ Himself.

This is, of course, a much higher stage than the one described before. Nowhere in his entire work does he speak about yet another path to the Phantom.

98. Verlag am Goetheanum, Dornach 2008.

99. Since this book was published by the same publisher who has printed all of J. v. Halle's books, there can be no doubt that this happened with her consent. Even she herself compares some of her visions with those of A. K. Emmerich in the Afterword to her book *Das Abendmahl* [The Last Supper]. Dornach 2006, as well as in the book *Vom Mysterium des Lazarus und der drei Johannes* [The Mystery of Lazarus and the Three Johns]. Dornach 2009.

100. The words quoted here were taken by P. Tradowsky from the book by L. RINSER: *Die Wahrheit über Konnersreuth* [The Truth about Konnersreuth]. Frankfurt am Main, 1954.

101. In her first book, J. v. Halle likewise speaks in a similar direction. She writes: 'It lies heavily on my heart to repeat a personal request: With all of these presentations, please do not place my person in the foreground, but rather that being who is working through the phenomena. Please consider me as a kind of "study medium"' (*Und wäre Er nicht auferstanden...* Verlag am Goetheanum, Dornach 2005, p. 57 G [p. 44 E]).

102. Since it is well-documented that many of J. v. Halle's descriptions correspond to those of A. K. Emmerich and T. Neumann (regarding this, see W. GARVELMANN, op. cit.), one would then logically have to arrive at the conclusion that the remarks of the two other stigmatics likewise constitute 'spiritual-scientific knowledge'.

103. See RUDOLF STEINER: *Die Goetheanum-Fenster* [The Goetheanum Windows] (GA K-12). Illustrated book,

Dornach 1996.

104. See, for example, the drawing from the lecture of 19 April 1924. In: *Wandtafelzeichnungen* [Blackboard Drawings], Vol. XV, p. 21.

105. About the spiritual significance of the Y-form, see further in S. O. PROKOFIEFF: *Und die Erde wird zur Sonne* [And the Earth Will Become a Sun]. Arlesheim 2012. Chapter 4: 'Das Kreuz auf Golgatha und der Weltenbaum' [The Cross on Golgotha and the World-Tree]. It is also the case that in Francis of Assisi's vision – which led to his stigmatization – Christ appeared to him crucified on the traditional form of the Cross, as Giotto has illustrated in the famous fresco in the Cappella Bardi in Florence. Inasmuch as in his book P. Tradowsky considers this painting to be an authentic reproduction of St. Francis' experiences, he should also accept the accuracy of his vision with regard to the form of the Cross.

106. GA 8, Chapter: 'Christianity and Pagan Wisdom', italics Rudolf Steiner.

107. Plato describes in his dialogue , in the passage that Rudolf Steiner repeats in the above-mentioned quote, precisely the intersection of two lines: +.

108. In German: *Chronik des lebendigen Christus.* Verlag Urachhaus, Stuttgart 1998. Rudolf Steiner's comment about A. K. Emmerich is found in the Introduction to the book. See further about this book in Appendix 3.

109. This makes it understandable why during the time of his final illness, Rudolf Steiner took nourishment daily until the very end, despite his loss of appetite and the great pain he experienced in relation to eating (for taking in any earthly substance had a poisonous effect on him). See ITA

WEGMAN: *An die Freunde* [To the Friends], 'Das Krankenlager, die letzten Tage und Stunden Dr. Steiners' [The Time of Illness, Dr. Steiner's Last Days and Hours], essay dated 19 April 1925. Arlesheim 1960.

110. In addition, the wound marks after Christ's Resurrection no longer belonged to His Resurrection body (Phantom), but to the aforementioned condensed etheric body. Rudolf Steiner explains this in the story of Thomas, who was permitted to touch Christ's scars. Rudolf Steiner says in this regard: 'Imagine that someone has a wound; then the etheric body contracts in a special way and forms a kind of scar. And in the specially contracted ether body, from which were drawn the constituent elements of the new ether body with which Christ clothed Himself, these wound-marks were made visible – appearing as peculiarly thickened spots, so that even Thomas could feel that he was dealing with a reality' (GA 130, 9 January 1912). This is also quite understandable, because the restored Phantom no longer contains physical material and thus can no longer give expression to wound marks, which themselves have an earthly-sensory origin.

111. H. BOOS-HAMBURGER: *Aus Gesprächen mit Rudolf Steiner über Malerei und einige Erinnerungen an die Zeit des ersten Goetheanum* [From Conversations with Rudolf Steiner about Painting and Some Memories from the Time of the First Goetheanum]. Basel 1954, p. 14. [English translation in: *Conversations about Painting with Rudolf Steiner. Recollections of Five Pioneers of the New Art Impulse.* SteinerBooks Publishing, Great Barrington, MA (US) 2008, p. 47.]

112. GA 131, 12 October 1911.

113. See S. O. PROKOFIEFF: *Und die Erde wird zur Sonne* [And the Earth Will Become a Sun]. Arlesheim 2012. Chapter 1, Supplementary section: 'Die fünf Agape-Organe des Auferstehungsleibes' [The Five Agape-Organs of the Resurrection Body].

114. In a contribution to J. v. Halle's first book, P. Tradowsky confirms this fact. He writes: 'In relation to the stigmata I would like once more to emphasize that the temporary stigmata appearing on the fourth stage of the Christian path of initiation, the Crucifixion, must be differentiated from the permanent stigmata caused by destiny' (*Und wäre Er nicht auferstanden...*, p. 40 G [p. 28 E]).

115. ROB STEINBUCH: *Stigmata im Lichte der Anthroposophie* [Stigmata in the Light of Anthroposophy]. Driebergen (NL) 2011.

116. See S. O. PROKOFIEFF: *The Mystery of the Resurrection in the Light of Anthroposophy*. Chapter 1: 'The Mystery of Golgotha and Spiritual Communion'. Temple Lodge 2010.

117. An Englishman now living in the USA.

118. Lindisfarne Books, Great Barrington, MA (US) 2009. [German edition: Informationslücke-Verlag, Basel (CH) 2009.]

119. In this regard, see the exact quotations of R. Powell in the book S. O. PROKOFIEFF: *The Case of Valentin Tomberg. Anthroposophy or Jesuitism?* Temple Lodge 1997. Ch. 12, pp. 126-128. [Original German edition: S. O. PROKOFIEFF / CH. LAZARIDÈS: *Der Fall Tomberg. Anthroposophie oder Jesuitismus.* Second, greatly expanded German edition of 1996, self-published, pp. 122 and 124.]

120. For further details, see the book cited in the previous note as well as S. O. PROKOFIEFF: *Valentin Tomberg and*

Anthroposophy. A Problematic Relationship. Temple Lodge 2005.

121. First printed in 1990 by Golden Stone Press; reprinted in 2000 by The Anthroposophic Press, New York.

122. Here I will only give a quote from the original text: 'The three stages represented by the spiritual teachers can be regarded as reflecting the activity of the Father, the Son, and the Holy Spirit, each of whom, in turn, is represented by a portion of the Bible: the Old Testament, the New Testament, and the *Apocalypse.* For the Old Testament is the *testament of the Father,* the New Testament is the *testament of the Son,* and the *Book of Revelation* is the *testament of the Holy Spirit*' (R. A. POWELL: *The Most Holy Trinosophia and the New Revelation of the Divine Feminine.* Anthroposophic Press 2000. Section: 'The Working Together of the Three Spiritual Teachers', italics R. Powell).

123. One need only once compare this with the way this theme has been unfolded by Rudolf Steiner, who constantly developed it further from 1910 to 1924, always adding new aspects to it.

124. R. POWELL: *Chronicle of the Living Christ.* Anthroposophic Press 1996. Just how problematic such convoluted presentations are is shown in the fact that R. Powell, in his calculations, simply takes for granted the assumption of A. K. Emmerich that the Turning Point of Time (the birth of Jesus) took place in the year 2 before our Christian era. In contrast, Rudolf Steiner fully recognized the beginning of the Turning Point of Time as established by Christianity, and confirmed this through his spiritual research.

Bibliography

The following list contains the sources of Rudolf Steiner's writings and lectures mentioned or cited in this book. They are ordered in accordance with the bibliography number within the complete edition of Rudolf Steiner's works (in German: *Gesamtausgabe*, designated as 'GA'). Where titles are given in German, this indicates that the volume has not yet been translated.

All quotations from The New Testament are based on *The New Testament. A Rendering by Jon Madsen*. Floris Books (UK) 2006.

Abbreviations:
Rudolf Steiner Press: RSP
Anthroposophic Press: AP
SteinerBooks Publishing: SB
Completion Press: CP

GA

8   *Christianity as Mystical Fact*, SB 2006.

12   *The Stages of Higher Knowledge*, AP 1967.

13   *An Outline of Occult Science*, Tr. H. Monges, AP 1972.

     Occult Science: An Outline, Tr. G. & M. Adams, RSP 2011.

     An Outline of Esoteric Science, Tr. C. Creeger, AP 1997.

14   *Four Mystery-Dramas*, SB 2007.

26 *Anthroposophical Leading Thoughts*, RSP 2007.

92 Die okkulten Wahrheiten alter Mythen und Sagen [The Occult Truths of Myths and Sagas].

94 *An Esoteric Cosmology*, SB 2008.

95 *Founding a Science of the Spirit*, RSP 1999.

97 *The Christian Mystery*, CP. Fragments appear in *The Christian Mystery*, AP 1998.

99 *Rosicrucian Wisdom*, RSP 2000.

100 Menschheitsentwickelung und Christus-Erkenntnis [Human Development and Christ Cognition].

103 *The Gospel of St. John*, AP 1984.

104 *The Apocalypse of St. John: Lectures on the Book of Revelation*, RSP 1985.

105 *Universe, Earth and Man.*

106 *Egyptian Myths and Mysteries*, AP 1971.

107 Geisteswissenschaftliche Menschenkunde [The Service of Spiritual Science to Humanity].
The lectures of 1 January and 22 March 1909 are included under the title *The Deed of Christ and the Opposing Spiritual Powers*, RSP 1976.
The lecture of 17 June 1909 is included in *The Being of Man and his Future Evolution*, RSP 1981.

109 *The Principle of Spiritual Economy: In Connection with Questions of Reincarnation*, RSP 1986.

112 *The Gospel of St. John and its Relation to the Other Three Gospels*, AP 1982.

117 Die tieferen Geheimnisse des Menschheitswerdens im Lichte der Evangelien [The Deeper Secrets of Human Becoming in the Light of the Gospels].
Some lectures are included in *Deeper Secrets of Human History in the Light of the Gospel of St. Matthew*, RSP 1985.

127 Die Mission der neuen Geistesoffenbarung [The Mission of the New Spirit-Revelation].
The lecture of 30 November 1911 is available in typescript Z437 under the title 'The Threefold Call from the Spiritual World'.

130 *Esoteric Christianity and the Mission of Christian Rosenkreutz*, RSP 2001.

131 *From Jesus to Christ*, RSP 2005.

133 *Earthly and Cosmic Man*, AP 1986.

138 *Initiation, Eternity and the Passing Moment*, AP 1980.

139 *The Gospel of St. Mark*, AP 2000.

143 Erfahrungen des Übersinnlichen. Die drei Wege der Seele zu Christus [Experiences of the Supersensory. Three Paths of the Soul to Christ].
Fragments are included in *Anthroposophy in Everyday Life*, AP 1995.
The lecture of 17 April 1912 is included in *Three Paths of the Soul to Christ*, AP 1942.
The lecture of 8 May 1912 is included in *Artistic Representation of Christ*.
The lecture of 17 December 1912 is published under the title *Love and its Meaning in the World*, SB 1998.

148 *The Fifth Gospel: From the Akashic Record*, RSP 2012.

155 *Christ and the Human Soul,* RSP 2008.

161 Wege der geistigen Erkenntnis und der Erneuerung künstlerischer Weltanschauung [Paths of Spiritual Cognition and the Renewal of an Artistic Worldview]. The lecture of 10 January 1915 is available in typescript Z273, 'Perception of the Nature of Thought'.

168 Die Verbindung zwischen Lebenden und Toten [The Connection between the Living and the Dead]. The lecture of 18 February 1916 is available in typescript NSL217, 'Concerning the Life Between Death and a New Birth'.

203 Die Verantwortung des Menschen für die Weltentwickelung [The Responsibility of the Human Being for World-Development]. The lectures of 1 January and 27 March 1921 are included in *The Festivals and their Meaning,* RSP 2008.

219 *Man and the World of Stars,* AP 1982.

237 *Karmic Relationships. Esoteric Studies,* Vol. III, RSP 2002.

238 *Karmic Relationships. Esoteric Studies,* Vol. IV, RSP 1983.

254 *The Occult Movement in the Nineteenth Century,* RSP 1973.

258 *The Anthroposophic Movement,* RSP 1993.

264 *From the History and Contents of the First Section of the Esoteric School, 1904 – 1914,* SB 2010.

293 *Study of Man: General Education Course,* RSP 2004. Also translated as *The Foundations of Human Experience,* AP 1996.

346 *The Book of Revelation and the Work of the Priest,* RSP 2008.